KEYNES IN ACTION

John Maynard Keynes died in 1946 but his ideas and his example remain relevant today. In this distinctive new account, Peter Clarke shows how Keynes's own career was not simply that of an academic economist, nor that of a modern policy advisor. Though rightly credited for reshaping economic theory, Keynes's influence was more broadly based and is assessed here in a rounded historical, political and cultural context. Peter Clarke re-examines the full trajectory of Keynes's public career from his role in Paris over the Versailles Treaty to Bretton Woods. He reveals how Keynes's insights as an economic theorist were rooted in his wider intellectual and cultural milieu including Bloomsbury and his friendship with Virginia Woolf as well as his involvement in government business. *Keynes in Action* uncovers a much more pragmatic Keynes whose concept of 'truth' needs to be interpreted in tension with an acknowledgement of 'expediency' in implementing public policy.

PETER CLARKE was elected a Fellow of the British Academy in 1989. His previous publications include *Hope and Glory: Britain 1900–2000* (2004), *The Locomotive of War: Money, Empire, Power, and Guilt* (2017) and studies on John Maynard Keynes including *The Keynesian Revolution in the Making, 1924–1936* (1988) and *Keynes* (2009).

KEYNES IN ACTION
Truth and Expediency in Public Policy

PETER CLARKE

University of Cambridge

 CAMBRIDGE
UNIVERSITY PRESS

CAMBRIDGE
UNIVERSITY PRESS

University Printing House, Cambridge CB2 8BS, United Kingdom

One Liberty Plaza, 20th Floor, New York, NY 10006, USA

477 Williamstown Road, Port Melbourne, VIC 3207, Australia

314–321, 3rd Floor, Plot 3, Splendor Forum, Jasola District Centre,
New Delhi – 110025, India

103 Penang Road, #05–06/07, Visioncrest Commercial, Singapore 238467

Cambridge University Press is part of the University of Cambridge.

It furthers the University's mission by disseminating knowledge in the pursuit of
education, learning, and research at the highest international levels of excellence.

www.cambridge.org
Information on this title: www.cambridge.org/9781009255011
DOI: 10.1017/9781009255028

© Peter Clarke 2023

First published 2023

Printed in the United Kingdom by TJ Books Limited, Padstow Cornwall

A catalogue record for this publication is available from the British Library.

Library of Congress Cataloging-in-Publication Data
NAMES: Clarke, P. F., author.
TITLE: Keynes in action : truth and expediency in public policy / Peter Clarke.
DESCRIPTION: New York, NY : Cambridge University Press, 2022. |
Includes bibliographical references and index.
IDENTIFIERS: LCCN 2022025079 | ISBN 9781009255011 (hardback) |
ISBN 9781009255028 (ebook)
SUBJECTS: LCSH: Keynes, John Maynard, 1883–1946. | Economists –
Great Britain – Biography. | Great Britain – Economic policy – 21st century.
CLASSIFICATION: LCC HB103.K47 C525 2022 |
DDC 330.15/6092 [B]–dc23/eng/20220818
LC record available at https://lccn.loc.gov/2022025079

ISBN 978-1-009-25501-1 Hardback

To Stefan Collini

CONTENTS

ACKNOWLEDGEMENTS

In different chapters I have expanded upon some previous research as published in specialist journals, notably 'Keynes and the *Manchester Guardian*'s Reconstruction Supplements,' *Annals of the Fondazione Luigi Einaudi* (Turin), vol. 51 (2–2017), 9–23; and 'We Can Conquer Unemployment: Lloyd George and Keynes', *Journal of Liberal History*, no. 77 (Winter 2012–13), 46–53. I have also drawn upon presentations that I made at the following international conferences: 'Global Crises, Policy Failures, and the Road to Prosperity', Franklin College Switzerland, Lugano, April 2010; 'Keynes's Relevance to the Contemporary World', Fondazione Luigi Einaudi, Turin, October 2016, a paper published as 'Rules and Discretion in the Making of Economic Policy,' *Annals of the Fondazione Luigi Einaudi* (Turin), vol. 51 (1–2017), 107–22; likewise a paper at the 'Economic Consequences of the Peace Conference', King's College, Cambridge, September 2019, organised by the Institute for New Economic Thinking, University of Cambridge; and some material on Bretton Woods for the conference 'Michal Kalecki and the Problem of International Equilibrium', under the auspices of the Permanent Representation of the Republic of Poland to the Organisation for Economic Co-operation and Development (OECD), Paris, September 2019. I am grateful to all those who invited me to make these contributions and, in the process, stimulated my own further thoughts. All estimates on relative purchasing power are taken from the invaluable website: MeasuringWorth.com.

I would like to thank my editor Michael Watson and Cambridge University Press for their readiness to publish this book; I have benefited from the shrewd comments of three anonymous advisors on the original submission, and from the help of Emily Plater and Natasha Whelan in production, likewise leading to beneficial amendment. In Cambridge the University Library was, as ever, an invaluable resource and the support of my two colleges, St John's and Trinity Hall, much appreciated. I owe a special debt to the readers on whom I inflicted drafts of some or all of my work in progress: in Cambridge, Terri Apter, Stefan Collini, David Newbery and John Thompson; on Pender Island, British Columbia, Richard G. Lipsey (for magisterial comment on Bretton Woods) and – throughout the long and restrictive months of the Covid pandemic – the constant support and critical comment of Maria Tippett.

Introduction

When John Maynard Keynes was born in 1883, Queen Victoria still had seventeen years to reign and, much to her disdain, the great Liberal hero Gladstone was again her Prime Minister. This was the world in which Maynard grew up, as a child of earnest, Liberal, Nonconformist parents in Harvey Road, Cambridge. His father, John Neville Keynes, was a university don, an economist and a dutiful administrator; whereas Florence, Maynard's much more vibrant and civic-minded mother, was to become the first woman mayor of Cambridge in 1932. Their house was unpretentiously comfortable, semi-detached and newly built, as the old university city expanded towards the railway station. Religious tests for College fellows had been removed by Gladstone's first government in 1871, thus allowing Neville (both father and son were known by their middle names) to become a Fellow of Pembroke College; but his decision to get married, once Cambridge's new statutes of 1882 made this possible, also lost him his college fellowship under the complex provisions now in place, though he retained a position in the expanding University bureaucracy. The Keynes family, with Florence having been an early student at the new women's college of Newnham, thus exemplified the changing status and character of the University, just as Harvey Road provided much-needed accommodation for a new type of academic family.

Maynard's first biographer, Roy Harrod, was perhaps too discreet by our standards about certain aspects of his life; but he was not wholly amiss in identifying 'the presuppositions of Harvey Road' as a formative influence – notably 'that the government of Britain was and would continue to be in the hands of an intellectual aristocracy using the method of persuasion' (Harrod 1951, 192–3). Keynes died prematurely in 1946, before either of his parents, but not before exerting great influence upon not only economic thought but upon many issues of public policy.

He lived in an era before it had become a cliché to say that the role of a public intellectual is to speak truth to power. But the problem that this phrase suggests was central to his career, which was an unusual one in many respects. Economists have long found it all too easy to appraise Keynes's analysis in terms of their own modern professional and academic ambit – often very different from his own. Conversely, historians looking at major policy questions in which Keynes was implicated have usually done so with more interest in the practical outcome than in his own perspective. In the process, 'Keynesian' has become a familiar adjective but often at the expense of losing sight of the person I call 'the historical Keynes'. The fact that he neither followed a strictly academic career path, nor simply adapted to an alternative role as an anonymous policy advisor, has implications that have been too little explored.

This remains the case despite the best efforts of his biographers. For Keynes has been lucky in this respect, inspiring a number of biographical studies which we can now take as our starting point. Roy Harrod, a distinguished economist himself, led the way in 1951 with a book full of insight though also, in that era, couched in deliberately evasive terms about aspects of his hero's life that it was not thought helpful to mention (especially not if the Americans were listening). In a later generation, uninhibited by such concerns, notably after the legal acceptance of homosexuality, Robert Skidelsky began afresh and, as his work expanded to three majestic volumes, offered a kaleidoscopic revisionist view. Meanwhile Donald Moggridge, steeled and sustained by his unrivalled archival mastery, which he had acquired in his role of guiding the invaluable thirty published volumes of Keynes's collected writings to completion, gave the world a weighty and authoritative tome of his own.

These landmark publications have both aided and stimulated authors in teasing out other biographical strands, with one notable book by Richard Davenport-Hines inventively exploring what he called 'the seven lives of John Maynard Keynes' to good effect. For example, it is indeed notable that Keynes's formative years had been spent with the friends who subsequently became identified as 'Bloomsbury', with their diverse and wide-ranging aesthetic interests. Moreover, the core of this group was the cohort of young Cambridge men whom Keynes had first met as fellow members of a cliquish – and ostensibly secret – society generally called 'the Apostles'. Though much of this is now well known, its significance remains contested; and we plainly have more to comprehend than simply the predestined career of an academic economist, however eminent.

If the great man was referred to as 'Professor Keynes' he would sometimes riposte that he would not accept the indignity without the emoluments. And it is not just pedantry to point out that he never actually became a 'professor' at Cambridge University, though obviously he could have done so if he had chosen otherwise. His only earned degree, achieved in the Cambridge Tripos examinations, had been a BA in Mathematics (all successful undergraduates in Cambridge, whether in the humanities or the sciences, graduate with this same Bachelor of Arts title). Keynes's subsequent formal tuition in economics had been cursory and informal; no question of a PhD, a degree that only arrived in Cambridge after 1920; and the dissertation that instead won Keynes a college fellowship was in philosophy. In modern academic terms, this all looks a bit amateurish.

Keynes did not follow the trajectory of a conventional modern academic career, partly through personal choice, but also because of structural changes during his lifetime. For the university system in England (leaving aside Scotland in this respect) was nothing like what we see today when half of all school-leavers go on to higher education. In 1914, to be sure, there were already about four thousand university students in London and over six thousand at provincial civic universities. But the pre-eminence of Oxford and Cambridge, together numbering nearly eight thousand (overwhelmingly male) undergraduates, seemed unassailable, with most of the wealth and patronage still in the hands of the ancient colleges. Conversely, the struggle for recognition of economics as a new academic discipline – a challenge in which John Neville Keynes had diligently supported the efforts of his former patron Alfred Marshall – was still a work in progress. There was an air of informality and improvisation in that era, unlike

4

the institutionalised structure familiar to later generations. The members of the Royal Economic Society, who constituted the subscribers to its periodical the *Economic Journal*, numbered only 563 when Keynes, at twenty-eight, took over as editor in 1911: a number that was to climb to 4,502 by the outbreak of the Second World War (Winch 2009, 356, 364). In a sense, Keynes grew up with the profession as we now see it; and today many of his own activities would be regarded as quite unprofessional.

In the world as it had looked to the young man brought up in Harvey Road, his parents' efforts in giving him a privileged education allowed him latitude in many dimensions that he only later came to appreciate as specific to a particular era. A scholarship to Eton College for his secondary education, secured with assiduous coaching in Cambridge and with the University's Vice Chancellor serving as one of the examiners, opened doors for him. Maynard's younger brother Geoffrey (later a distinguished surgeon) was sent to Rugby School – the days of his youth, so he recalled, 'lived under the shadow of a far more forceful and intellectual character than my own' (Keynes 1981, 19). Maynard later acted as best man when Geoffrey married Margaret Darwin (granddaughter of the great Charles) in 1917; their sister Margaret Keynes, likewise overshadowed, had already married A. V. Hill, a Fellow of Trinity, who was to win the Nobel Prize for Physiology in 1922. The Keyneses became part of an inbred Cambridge elite. Maynard's youthful homosexual adventures can be seen as one kind of rebellion; his later marriage to an exotic Russian ballerina as another. He always liked to have the best of both worlds.

Maynard's application for a university place at Cambridge had dangled before him the temptations of Trinity, simultaneously the college of Newton (always an iconic figure for him) and also the wealthiest in the university. But the attractions of King's prevailed: a college with historic institutional links that still reserved half of its entrance scholarships for boys from Eton. Happily, John Maynard Keynes now became one of these, adept in his performance not only in mathematics but adding to his lustre (and his emoluments) by proficiency in classics. The college obligingly shifted the date of the examination to allow young Maynard to secure combined scholarships that gave him not only £80 a year (say, £8,000 in today's money) but also free rooms and tuition. This was meritocracy with an insider twist – a lifelong theme in Keynes's career.

Keynes's uniquely long tenure as Editor of the *Economic Journal*, in that era probably the most respected forum in the world for discussions of economic theory, later served to reinforce his authority and influence within the burgeoning academic profession worldwide. Alongside all this, for at least thirty years Keynes sustained a close, persistent and often influential role in shaping public policy. He had been a civil servant in London, at the India Office, before he became a don in Cambridge. In the First World War he served in the Treasury in a temporary position; and it was in this role that he went to Paris in 1919 while Lloyd George, as British Prime Minister, negotiated the peace terms subsequently imposed upon Germany. Here was the origin of the book that made Keynes famous, *The Economic Consequences of the Peace* (1919), published in Britain in December 1919 and a few weeks later in its American edition, following his resignation in the

previous summer in protest at Lloyd George's actions over
the reparations demanded from Germany.

Keynes's widely read tract precipitated him to international fame, as much in the United States as in Europe. His
career was nothing if not controversial: first over the Versailles
Treaty and reparations, then over Britain's return to the gold
standard in 1925, and with an ongoing concern in both explaining and remedying the high levels of unemployment that
beset not only Britain but most of the world by the 1930s. That
Keynes was recalled to government service in Britain during
the Second World War was in a sense predictable. As a result,
in the 1940s he directed his energies not only to coping with
Britain's immediate financial exigencies but also to envisaging
a new international economic order. Keynes's work in preparing this sort of agenda for the Bretton Woods conference of
1944, increasingly enmeshed with negotiating a post-war financial settlement between the impoverished sterling area and the
now dominant dollar economy of the United States, became
the final task of his life. These are all themes and episodes that
I explore in this book; and in doing so I hope to bring out the
significance of an abiding issue that needs addressing explicitly.

***

What is truth? How do we know what we think we know?
With what degrees of certainty can we hold our beliefs? How
should we act? How far should we feel constrained in our
actions by their likely consequences? How can we perceive in
advance the likelihood of those consequences? How far can
we trust such perceptions? Such questions frame *A Treatise on
Probability* (1921), the first academic book published by Keynes,

who treated them there with relentless scholarly rigour. But the questions themselves inevitably provoke concerns within a much broader and more practical context, with implications for issues of economic policy and political action alike.

I am not only concerned with the status of truth in Keynes's thinking but also with the claims of expediency in resolving issues of public policy, where other considerations might well impose their own priorities. In such a perspective, it may be simplistic to deride the efforts of those charged with political or economic responsibilities for 'selling out', or for 'betrayal', or for 'covering up' or for 'lying'. Expediency, discretion, pragmatism and common sense may have their own legitimacy, not least in judging actions by their likely consequences. Do we need, then, a process of unmasking to reveal the implicit motives that silently moved Keynes in some of his actions in policy-making?

These are matters on which the thirty volumes of the *Collected Writings of John Maynard Keynes*, to which all scholars are now indebted, can offer us different kinds of perspective; and I shall make citations from twenty-nine of them in the chapters that follow. But many assumptions have changed since the time when this worthy project was first conceived as the Royal Economic Society's tribute to a great economist who was claimed as one of their own – a point that can be illustrated even by an anomaly in the way that one of the volumes is numbered, as soon becomes apparent when they are all stacked in line along the bookshelf.

The first volume duly reprints *Indian Currency and Finance*, originally published in 1913, which was an indirect offshoot of Keynes's initial professional career as a civil servant in the India Office from 1906 to 1908. It is a work that displays not only his facility in expounding the subject with theoretical rigour but also his evident expertise in the actual workings of the system of public finance in British India. The exposition is relieved on occasion by the sort of dry wit prized in the higher civil service in Whitehall. This is sometimes turned against its begetters, for instance in one remark on how 'the natural instincts of the Treasury officials became uncontrollable, and respect for the independence of the India Office had to be abandoned' (JMK 1:46). Nor are the bankers spared comment on 'certain, almost Gilbertian, characteristics calculated to bring the name and profession of banking into derision or disrepute' (JMK 1:162). And even when such an exalted figure as the Secretary of State for India is quoted, Keynes's cursory comment – 'no need to name him, it is the eternal secretary of state speaking' – suggests some lack of awe for his former political masters (JMK 1:165). But these are rare flashes of mischief in a dense and austere account.

The second volume of Keynes's *Collected Writings* reprints his *Economic Consequences*, as originally published at the end of 1919. The adjacent third volume reprints *A Revision of the Treaty*, a sequel published in January 1922; but that was not the only work of revision on which Keynes had meanwhile been engaged. For his new book on the Treaty was written, rather quickly and drawing on his published journalism, just after Keynes had spent much of the autumn of 1920 and the spring of 1921 in preparing a major scholarly tome for publication.

A Treatise on Probability was published in August 1921 – but numbered by the editors of the *Collected Writings* in the early 1970s as the eighth volume, thus awkwardly appended, out of sequence, to what was then considered the relevant *oeuvre* of Keynes as an economist. In the half century or so since that decision on scholarly republication was taken, our perspectives have shifted a good deal; and it is now generally recognised that the young Keynes was not simply 'a philosopher' who subsequently decided to refashion a different career as 'an economist'. Instead, we have a fertile academic literature to draw upon in showing us that his concern with the concept of probability stayed with him as a lifelong intellectual concern. The problem here was thus stubbornly persistent, but whether his response to it was consistent has been a matter of scholarly contention.

Probability was, as we now know, a detailed revision of drafts that dated back to the two dissertations that Keynes had submitted for competitive research fellowships at King's College, Cambridge, in 1907 (unsuccessfully) and in 1908 with eventual success in getting him elected as a Fellow. It is apparent, then, that he had at least twelve years to refine his drafts – and very likely about fifteen years from the moment when he had first focussed on these abstruse epistemological problems, with their implications about the status of our knowledge, not least when making moral decisions.

Admittedly Keynes's time had meanwhile often been pre-empted for more pressing concerns: learning as well as teaching economics in Cambridge; serving on the Royal Commission on Indian Finance and Currency (1913–14) for which his *Indian Currency and Finance* had so obviously prepared him; and then in his career as a temporary civil servant in the Treasury, dealing with the external finance of the war;

and, after the Armistice, serving in Paris as the Treasury's official representative during the peace negotiations. One thing
had led to another in the course of this busy life, sometimes,
as in his appointment to the Indian Royal Commission, fairly
predictably. Unpredictably, however, Keynes's second book,
the *Economic Consequences*, had suddenly become a world-
famous polemic.

Only after this had been published, then, did Keynes
find time to return to the academic issues of probability with
which he had grappled for so long. He fully realised that these
scholarly writings, revised through many drafts, would attract
the attention of only a tiny fraction of the readership of his
controversial writings on the Treaty. But the problems that he
worked through with such care, and took such pains to expound
within a tight methodological frame, were not simply compart-
mentalised in a separate part of his own capacious brain. His
thinking now inevitably bore the marks and the burdens of his
own experience – yet he was also conceptually constrained by
the existing shape of a revised fellowship dissertation from 1908
which had indeed been set up in proof copies by his publishers (Macmillan) before the First World War had intervened.
His task had thus been left over from another era, one of which
Keynes had written feelingly, with an almost Proustian nostalgia,
in the opening chapter of the *Economic Consequences*. 'What an
extraordinary episode in the economic progress of man that age
was which came to an end in August 1914!' (JMK 2:6).

***

By January 1922, then, three books from this busy author
had appeared in little more than two years; and though there

were obvious contrasts between them, they each had a distinctive viewpoint on a common problem: the nature and status of truth. In some contexts it seems axiomatic that truth-telling is the only right and proper course; academic inquiry, research and exposition all rest on this common basis of good faith. This is equally true in mathematics, in philosophy, in classics, in history and in economics – each of them now well-defined academic disciplines in which the young Keynes had evinced more than passing interest.

Yet was it always prudent to observe such rigour in politics? And which of his hats was the young Keynes wearing? Austin Robinson, long a close colleague in Cambridge and on the *Economic Journal*, was forthright in affirming that 'his absorbing interest in politics and government made Keynes, in the very best sense of those words, a political economist' (Robinson 1947, 10). So was it sometimes necessary, as the old civil service cliché has it, to be economical with the truth? And though Keynes may have resigned from the British Treasury in 1919, did that absolve him from a duty of confidentiality that might inhibit a simple impulse to tell all?

Here was a charge that Keynes had already faced – and faced down – from two friendly critics who had privately expressed their unease over how the *Economic Consequences* would be received. Arthur Salter, an economist now working for the Reparations Commission set up under the Treaty, had been one. In October 1919, two months before the book's publication, Keynes had responded to Salter that 'it is such a hopeless business trying to calculate the psychological effect of one's actions; and I have come to feel that the best thing in all the circumstances is to speak the truth as bluntly as one can' (JMK 17:6–7). He likewise wrote to the South African leader Jan Christiaan Smuts, currently Keynes's most prominent political ally, a few weeks later, when it was already too late to change anything in the printed book, saying that 'I personally despair of results from anything but violent and ruthless truth-telling – that will work *in the end*, even if slowly' (JMK 17:7–8, italics in original).

There is more than one difficulty in taking these affirmations literally, as the truth about truth. Writing in in the closing months of 1921, a couple of years after his *Economic Consequences* had first propelled him to a peak of public recognition, Keynes chose to begin its sequel, *A Revision of the Treaty* (1922), with a short chapter called 'The State of Opinion', which is revealing in more senses than one. For in these pages Keynes now offered an apology of sorts to Lloyd George, by claiming that he faced a new problem in an era when 'public passions and public ignorance play a part in the world of which he who aspires to lead a democracy must take account'. Hence Keynes now outlined 'a plausible defence' for Lloyd George's decisions in Paris on the grounds that 'the Peace of Versailles was the best momentary settlement which the demands of the mob and the characters of the chief actors conjoined to permit'. Not 'the best settlement', then, but one that, with the qualification of 'momentary', implied further opportunities, which only the passage of time could offer, for subsequent efforts 'in avoiding or moderating the dangers'. Policy was thus a complex process, to be judged by its ultimate results. Keynes now suggested the possibility 'that this is the best of which a democracy is capable – to be jockeyed, humbugged, cajoled along the right road. A preference for truth or for sincerity *as a method* may be a prejudice based on some aesthetic or personal standard, inconsistent, in politics, with practical good' (JMK 3:1–2, italics in original).

One obvious political problem about telling the truth, then, was that it might be incompatible with satisfying public opinion. *A Revision of the Treaty* asserted that 'there are, in the present times, two opinions: not, as in former ages, the true and the false, but the outside and the inside'. Mr Gladstone, who 'dropped no mask in private life', was dead (though no doubt still mourned in Harvey Road). Now, outside opinion was voiced by politicians and newspapers, while the inside opinion was expressed in limited circles by those in the know, who realised that 'appearances can no longer be kept up behind the scenes' (JMK 3:3). This introduced an allegedly new element of conscious hypocrisy into the problem of formulating public policy, raising an awkward question of exactly how much calculated deception or evasion was politically expedient. Some modern historians who seek to extenuate the making of the Treaty as a provisional exercise, susceptible of beneficial amendment when wartime passions had cooled, should perhaps acknowledge this pedigree for their revisionist insights.

Hence the concrete conclusion to Keynes's chapter – applied to the Treaty as signed in June 1919 but now viewed in the changed circumstances of some two years later – that 'this element of make-believe has ceased to be politically necessary; that outside opinion is now ready for inside opinion to disclose, and act upon, its secret convictions; and that it is no longer an act of futile indiscretion to speak sensibly in public' (JMK 3:5). The point that Keynes chose to raise explicitly here, moreover, was not simply a belated perspective, born of his official government experience: it was also informed by his own academic studies and his own ponderously long-considered reflections on the status of truth.

Hence the tension between the purported stance of Keynes's *Economic Consequences* and the ostensibly more relaxed criteria that are subsequently suggested, a couple of years later, in the same author's *Revision of the Treaty*. A crude way to describe the difference between these two books is to say that the *Economic Consequences* is motivated by an axiomatic belief in the value of truth whereas, when the *Revision* discloses some second thoughts, it is to point to the virtue of expediency – which often sounds simply like common sense.

There is a famous episode in the history of economic thought – 'das Adam Smith Problem' – that turns on whether what the great economist wrote in one of his books is a contradiction of what he wrote in another; or whether the two can happily be reconciled, which is what most intellectual historians would argue today. Likewise, I am not alone in thinking that the two books that Keynes published about the Treaty, though differing in focus, offer compatible visions on the role of expediency. For in the *Economic Consequences* Keynes had already set out the criteria that the book proposed to apply: 'It was the task of the peace conference to honour engagements and to satisfy justice; but not less to re-establish life and to heal wounds' (JMK 2:16). So first he stated a basically legal criterion, for the Allies to fulfil specific contractual obligations in the Armistice that they had signed with Germany, reinforced by invocation of a broader sense of what was morally right. This in itself set a taxing standard for fulfilment. But this criterion was immediately qualified by a more functional sense of pragmatism, explicitly appealing to prudence as well as magnanimity.

Let us take one concrete example. Some of the expectations fostered by the Treaty – especially rhetorical expectations of the Allies' eventual financial benefit from reparations – would prove to be temporary delusions. These would pass, bursting like bubbles. But the clauses demanding German delivery of coal as reparations, nourishing hopes of both French and Italian financial solvency, were more specifically based. These were real and concrete stipulations, but hardly feasible unless German miners could be recompensed for actually digging the coal itself. In his analysis, Keynes did not deny the merits of the French and Italian claims, simply saying: 'It is a case where particular interests and particular claims, however well founded in sentiment or in justice, must yield to sovereign expediency' (JMK 2:60). The claim for 'expediency' to override 'justice' is explicit here; elsewhere it is implicit in some of Keynes's own transactions in Paris.

His use of this language of expediency surely derives from Edmund Burke, whose influence on the young Keynes was established in important publications by scholars in the 1980s and 1990s. Their key source was the substantial prize essay on Edmund Burke that Keynes had written in 1904, in which the salience of 'Expediency' is explicitly affirmed. As the young Keynes put it, this followed from Burke's 'preference for peace over truth', a sort of justification, however, about which he professed himself dubious, instead affirming (in another essay of 1905): 'The advantage of truth lies in the greater stability that it gives' (Moggridge 1992, 127). Yet this

16

was an appeal to a balance of advantage that might in principle be changed on pragmatic grounds, since it remained subject to 'the supremacy of expediency' in Keynes's eyes (Fitzgibbons 1988, 56–7). And the utilitarian frame of Keynes's commendation of Burke, as shown in his readiness to champion 'expediency against abstract right', captures the overriding sense of his argument at this time (O'Donnell 1989, 284–5; Skidelsky 1983, 155–6).

Such had been the contentions of a clever Cambridge undergraduate at the beginning of his final year (1904–5) before sitting the Tripos examination in Mathematics; and their status in governing his subsequent thinking should not be exaggerated. Nonetheless, we misread the *Economic Consequences* if we simply take it as a paean to truth and justice at all costs. After all, on quitting Paris in early June 1919, Keynes had written to Lloyd George: 'I've gone on hoping even through these last dreadful weeks that you'd find some way to make of the treaty a just and expedient document' (JMK 16:469).

Rather than presenting a condemnation of the Treaty in absolute terms, the *Economic Consequences* can be read as a finely calibrated exercise in weighing morality against expediency in the scales of justice. Inflexible appeals to truth were thus, in themselves, sometimes inadequate in achieving expedient solutions. In the early pages of the *Economic Consequences* President Woodrow Wilson is introduced as the central figure, initially enjoying 'a prestige and a moral influence throughout the world unequalled in history' (JMK 2:24). But a warning is signalled about his efficaciousness since 'in fact the President had thought out nothing; when it came to practice his ideas were nebulous and incomplete'. Hence the fatal flaw in his Fourteen Points. 'He could have preached a sermon on any of them or have addressed a stately prayer to the Almighty for their fulfilment; but he could not frame their concrete application to the actual state of Europe' (JMK 2:27). Keynes does not mock this prophetic stance so much as deride Wilson's lack of either executive capacity or flexibility in negotiation. 'Compromise was inevitable, and never to compromise on the essential, very difficult' (JMK 2:29).

Just how difficult becomes a major theme of the book – the root of Wilson's personal tragedy. 'Although compromises were now necessary, he remained a man of principle and the Fourteen Points a contract absolutely binding upon him. He would do nothing that was not honourable; he would do nothing that was not just and right; he would do nothing that was contrary to his great profession of faith'. Hence his fatal dependence on 'all the intellectual apparatus of self-deception' necessary to square the circle (JMK 2:31–2). These are the standards, then, by which the Versailles Treaty is judged: not whether it was a compromise but by 'the quality which chiefly distinguishes this transaction from all its historical predecessors – its insincerity' (JMK 2:40).

There could hardly have been more at stake; but the battle had been lost, in Keynes's account, by the time of his own resignation. And if it was wrong, both morally and legally, for the Allies to redefine the costs of the war as reparations rather than indemnities, the consequences were serious. 'Apart from other aspects of the transaction, I believe that the campaign for securing out of Germany the general costs of the war was one of the most serious acts of political unwisdom for which our statesmen have ever been responsible' (JMK 2:92). It was a gross blunder to be measured by its equally serious consequences. The financial expectations raised on German capacity to pay 'were so very remote from the truth that a slight distortion of figures was no use, and it was necessary to ignore the facts entirely. The resulting unveracity was fundamental. On a basis of so much falsehood it became impossible to erect any constructive financial policy which was workable' (JMK 2:94).

Such a gross sacrifice of truth thus offended the criterion of expediency. In this sense Keynes could claim justification either way in condemning a demand upon Germany that was simultaneously unjustified on legal grounds and impracticable in its economic effect. 'Some preach it in the name of justice', he wrote of the Treaty's terms. 'In the great events of man's history, in the unwinding of the complex fates of nations, justice is not so simple' (JMK 2:142). The Treaty terms, he argued, would not last: 'They do not square with human nature or agree with the spirit of the age'. It was a prediction, he suggested, in which 'expediency and generosity agree together' in recommending a magnanimous policy (JMK 2:179). Perhaps Keynes too easily conflated the criteria that he applied here; and, as we shall see, in judging the actions of the policy-makers in Paris in 1919 he did not always tell the whole truth about his own part.

Nor did he in other, later episodes; but the tension between truth and expediency remains a potent if often undeclared theme, stubbornly recurrent in Keynes's career, as will be apparent in later chapters of this book. Here I am often building upon, or commenting upon, the work of earlier writers (as some of my citations above already suggest). And I am not simply presenting the case for the defence, as will perhaps become clear in the two chapters with which I begin, dealing with Keynes's own role and responsibility in creating one of the most explosive provisions of the Versailles Treaty: the so-called War Guilt Clause.

What Really Happened at Paris?
Keynes and Dulles

The devastating effects upon Europe of the First World War can hardly be exaggerated. We think first of the death toll among the millions of young men who fought each other, not only on the western front in France but on the less commemorated eastern front, or on that between Italy and the Habsburg Empire. A vast number of others, men, women and children alike, perished through violence, famine and disease; the influenza epidemic has excited new attention in the era of Covid. Great empires collapsed: the Romanovs first but then inexorably the Habsburgs, the Hohenzollerns and the Ottomans. The two leading European Allies, Britain and France, eventually claimed victory and it is true that the peace treaties aggrandised them territorially, especially in the Middle East – with long-term results that we are still confronting today.

But the only real winner was the United States, especially in establishing its economic supremacy in a way that challenged *all* Europeans, though initially it fell to the victors among them to remake the world after this 'war to end war'. The fact that the United States, having acted as the supreme arbiter at the peace conference in Paris in 1919, later refused to ratify the resulting treaties was a body-blow to liberal hopes. The League of Nations had been the brainchild of

President Wilson and was set up as an organisation premised on American leadership, yet it subsequently became a forum from which the United States excluded itself.

If John Maynard Keynes made his name in writing about the economic consequences of these successive events, it was for deep-seated reasons, endowing his work with more than transient polemical status. It was the war that had brought him into a key role in the British Treasury, where he became largely responsible for the external finance of the British war effort. This was still nominally conducted under the gold standard, by means of huge dollar loans, some of which were in reality on behalf of Britain's allies (France, Italy, Russia, Belgium, Serbia, etc.) since their own credit rating failed to satisfy the Americans. In this way Keynes acquired a unique perspective on the issue of war debts, not least because of his own (largely unacknowledged) responsibility for running them up on such a large scale. Equally obvious is the link with the 'reparations' demanded from Germany by the victors in Paris, much to Keynes's disapproval. Here, then, lay the reasons for this young British Treasury official to resign his important government post in the early summer of 1919 and devote his time to the composition of a short book published at the end of that year.

The Economic Consequences of the Peace was no mere economic analysis by a technical expert. It was a polemical work of great artistry and eloquence that took the world by storm. Keynes's close friend Lytton Strachey, the author of the recent bestseller *Eminent Victorians* (1918), could hardly have bettered the literary effect of some of the early chapters of the *Economic Consequences*, with their feline portraits of Lloyd George and Wilson, both of them professed liberals in whom Keynes was now bitterly disappointed. Accordingly, in both Britain and the United States the *Economic Consequences* found ready admirers, especially but not exclusively on the left. In France, conversely, it faced scorn, not least because it was widely perceived as pro-German. And in Germany, it is true, Keynes was more deeply implicated in the machinations to subvert any real fulfilment of the economic clauses than he cared to admit at the time. Certainly his arguments were soon put to work in justifying the 'innocence campaign' against German liability for reparations, as demanded under the terms of the Peace Treaty signed at Versailles in 1919.

These terms were controversial from the start. In particular the demand for heavy reparations from Germany, tied to Article 231 of the Treaty – the 'War Guilt Clause' – was seen as crucial. This clause had been scorned from the outset by Count Brockdorff-Rantzau, the leader of the German delegation, when the draft treaty was first presented to the Germans on 7 May 1919. It was a month later that Lloyd George, as leader of the British Empire delegation, and now belatedly seeking concessions from his American and French counterparts, reported to them: 'One of my financial experts has just left us, because he finds the terms too hard' (PWW 60:315). This veiled reference to the resignation of Keynes, a couple of days after his thirty-sixth birthday, was not lost on members of the French delegation (who generally despised Keynes); but it was the younger members of the United States delegation who had most cause to regret the departure of someone they had come to regard as a comrade-in-arms in battling for moderation in the proposed peace terms.

Most of this had happened behind closed doors. It was, above all, Keynes's subsequent actions that threw open the doors and let in the daylight – or so it seemed at the time to many Anglo-American liberals. After resigning his temporary civil service status, Keynes went back to academic life in Cambridge; but his first task that summer was to revisit the story of the negotiations in Paris for a wider public. With great artistry, his account highlighted the interaction between Lloyd George, the French premier Georges Clemenceau and the American President Woodrow Wilson. The publication at the end of 1919 of the *Economic Consequences* achieved its extraordinary impact partly because an expectant readership on both sides of the Atlantic was already waiting to hear the worst. Keynes's tract simultaneously broke the dam on information about the Paris conference and, throughout the English-speaking world, came to define the terms of a debate, primarily focussed on reparations, that has lasted for over a century.

The book had sold 18,500 copies in Britain by April 1920; the American edition sold 70,000 copies within a year. And inevitably such a controversial tract provoked other publications. There were predictably hostile responses from former members of the French delegation, and more ambivalent attempts, as we shall see, to sustain the official American point of view on issues that remained in the forefront of public debate. In the course of time, with an iterative process that successively released more documentary evidence over the next two decades, some of the gaping holes in the account given in the *Economic Consequences* were successively revealed – though with curiously little damage to the author's reputation.

What Really Happened at Paris was the emblematic title of a series of public lectures given in Philadelphia and published in 1921 under the editorial aegis of President Wilson's former advisor, Colonel Edward House (with aid from the young historian Charles Seymour). This title posed a question that still needs a satisfactory answer. We need to pay more attention to the complex interaction of Anglo-American arguments about what was at stake when it came to negotiating a peace treaty in the French capital during the first half of 1919, following the Armistice negotiated with Germany in November 1918. Some of the issues were indeed matters of economic analysis, as the title of Keynes's tract might lead prospective readers to suppose – though such readers would soon find themselves grappling with implicit moral questions. And some crucial issues were characterised by the United States delegation in specifically legal terms, in a way perhaps natural within the ambit of American political culture.

This helps to explain the salient role played in Paris by the young John Foster Dulles. He is chiefly remembered today for his role in the 1950s as Secretary of State in the Eisenhower administration, identified in a highly politicised way as a right-wing Republican and cold warrior. But his early career was as a lawyer, recruited to the Paris peace conference at the age of thirty – five years younger than even Keynes – and acting as the chief legal advisor to the Economic Section of the US delegation for eight months in 1919. He was thus involved in almost daily meetings of the 'experts' who had to advise on the issue of reparations, in practice working closely with the British experts, which brought him into close contact with Keynes. It was not just their professed expertise, however defined, that brought them together but a largely common political outlook on the big issues.

The *Economic Consequences* had abundant success – perhaps excessive success – in directing attention to what the author saw as the salient issues in the story it told; but as a history of what happened in Paris, it contains some significant silences, which merit further exploration. Some of these silences concern the role of Dulles, whose name does not appear in the *Economic Consequences*. But after its publication, this omission was duly remedied during the subsequent controversy. In the course of time, Dulles's side of the case did not go by default, least of all for lack of evidence, as might be expected of a lawyer who, in a scholarly biographer's words, 'had saved a small mountain of documents from the Paris Peace Conference' (Pruessen 1982, 515). In short, much of the relevant evidence in this is not actually hidden, or sealed in inaccessible archives. Instead, answers can be retrieved from an attentive reading of published documents – provided, of course, that we pose the right questions.

At the time of the publication of the *Economic Consequences* in December 1919, the book's authority was reinforced by the fact that much of it was evidently based upon insider information. Keynes had been working as a civil servant for the British government and was therefore bound by the rules and conventions of confidentiality. He acknowledged this in the preface, with the claim that the grounds on which he based his criticism were 'entirely of a public character, and are based on facts known to the whole world' (JMK 2:xv). This is stretching the truth somewhat, given the extent to which Chapters 4 and 5, amounting to over half the book, drew upon confidential government documents to which he had had privileged access. Indeed this is the reason for some subsequent claims that Keynes was, in effect, purloining assessments of the scope and impact of reparations from colleagues who had worked with him in ways that he was obviously not free to acknowledge. Alternatively, this is evidence that he was purveying a Treasury view of the problem without overtly affronting the rather ill-defined code of that era.

Keynes may not have been guilty of a technical infringement of the rules but his former chief as Chancellor of the Exchequer, Austen Chamberlain, was not alone in privately expressing some qualms as to whether the author had abused his official status. But the conventions were not well defined at the time; and almost all of what was recycled in the *Economic Consequences* was from what Keynes himself had drafted, leaving no aggrieved parties over the copyright. One way or another, Keynes had a good alibi for picking and choosing what he revealed and what, for the moment at least, he chose to suppress.

Nonetheless, readers of the *Economic Consequences* – if it were their only source of information on the peace conference – would gain a very curious impression of what really happened in Paris. The centrepiece of the book's account is the famous third chapter, simply entitled 'The Conference', presenting its exquisite satire on the workings of the Council of Four. Of these four leaders, Orlando of Italy is barely mentioned, which is a fair reflection of his marginal role, exacerbated by his own misjudged decision to withdraw at one stage. It is thus the interaction between Clemenceau, Lloyd George and Wilson that forms the crux of the story.

The author was criticised at the time by two French participants, Paul Mantoux and André Tardieu. The two of them were closely associated, as trusted officials working for Clemenceau, who had brought in Mantoux (whose English was impeccable) as interpreter, first for the Supreme War Council, then for the Council of Ten – initially set up as the inner circle of the major Allies represented at the peace conference – and ultimately for the Council of Four from 24 March 1919 onwards. Mantoux's notes of the meetings of the Council of Four happily survive as a key document – despite Tardieu losing one of the two original copies in the 1930s – with a continuing relevance signalled by their publication in 1992 in an English translation. (This was produced by the editors of Woodrow Wilson's papers, which is the more accessible edition that I cite in my quotations in this chapter and the next since their text is identical in both versions). Mantoux's credentials account for the seriousness of the allegations that surfaced in the early 1920s, originating from him, that Keynes was purporting to describe at first hand a personal interaction within the Council of Four that he could not have witnessed. The substance of these charges, which had quickly (and inaccurately) been relayed through American sources sympathetic to Wilson, was exhaustively laid to rest when the relevant volume of the Keynes papers was published in 1977 (JMK 17:101–9). But laying such ghosts to rest is an inherently intractable task.

Now Mantoux worked with the British official Maurice Hankey in compiling the official minutes and, as the editors of Mantoux's texts affirm, 'neither version contradicts nor impugns the other' (Link and Boemeke 1992, xvi). For present purposes, one irony about Mantoux's allegations is that it is often *his own notes* of the meetings of the Council of Four, or the official version produced with Hankey, that show Keynes to have been in attendance on relevant occasions and, on certain occasions, to have spoken himself, notably in dialogue with Wilson. Modern critics of Keynes have often followed Mantoux's cue in claiming that the *Economic Consequences* magnified the author's own role. But, as I hope to demonstrate, the real charge that could be made against Keynes is not that he was an ignorant outsider but actually the opposite: that the *Economic Consequences* serves to obfuscate just how closely the author was himself implicated in some crucial dealings, notably between the British and American delegations, in producing the final proposals and treaty texts on reparations.

The fact is that the Council of Four, replacing the Council of Ten, was itself a late development in the procedure of the Allied negotiations in Paris, which had commenced in January 1919. During the opening month or so, in deference to Wilson's priorities, the peace conference had been structured around the need to produce a blueprint for the League of Nations, a grand project that mainly enlisted the enthusiasm of the American and British delegations, especially the junior members. Clemenceau barely concealed his sense of frustration; Lloyd George dissimulated more tactfully. Hence the weeks that passed, with Wilson himself in the chair for League business, while Lloyd George and Clemenceau largely delegated this matter to others. This gave great prominence within the British Empire delegation to Jan Christiaan Smuts of South Africa, whose role in developing policy on

mandates for former German colonies was particularly notable. It is highly pertinent that Smuts came to acquire such status as a liberal hero.

***

In the course of these proceedings many links were formed
during January and February between the American and
British delegations, especially at the level of the younger
officials who had been seconded to Paris, like Dulles on reparations, or Keynes on Treasury business. For example, the
diary of Harold Nicolson of the British Foreign Office, aged
thirty-three at the time, confirms the ambit within which
these amicable anglophone contacts were established. 'French
furious at English being accepted as an official language', he
noted drily on 16 January (Nicolson 1933, 240). 'The ground
work we have done with the Americans is of great value', he
wrote on 8 February, after working for a couple of days with
Charles Seymour of the US delegation, the aide and confidant
of Colonel House (whose diary Seymour later edited for publication in the 1920s) (Nicolson 1933, 259–60).

Keynes's closest relationship was with Norman
Davis, an American Reparations Commissioner, now in
the US Treasury. Davis can be called a smooth operator in
many senses of that term. Five years older than Keynes, he
had amassed considerable wealth through business opera-
tions in Cuba that long dogged his name and may have subsequently deterred Franklin Roosevelt from appointing him
as Secretary of State in 1933. Already in 1919, the pattern had
been set. Davis's acknowledged charm and his progressive
credentials in supporting Wilson evidently appealed to one

side of Keynes's personality; but so did the racy appetite for playing the markets, as seen in Keynes's youthful relish for his own ventures in currency speculation and the mischievous temptations of exploiting financial opportunities. They evidently sensed such affinities, quickly establishing a close working relationship that broke through the barriers of strict diplomatic etiquette.

As early as 14 January 1919, Keynes explained to his Treasury bosses: 'In all the meetings I have been to so far Norman Davis and I privately concerted our policy together beforehand and I hear that this sort of thing is going on in other quarters also' (JMK 16:388). This was even before the two of them, shortly afterwards, found themselves on a train to Trier (or Trèves, on the German frontier) and discovered their mutual dedication to playing bridge, which Keynes often did for quite large stakes. 'We played almost continuously day and night during the whole of our journey and during the whole of our three days' stop at Trèves, except when we were actually in conference with Germans', Keynes revealed later (JMK 10:393). And when he finally came to depart from Paris, having resigned, it was to Davis that he wrote – 'I am slipping away on Saturday from this scene of nightmare' – setting up a lunch appointment for 'one last talk with you' (JMK 16:471). To the end of the conference, then, such personal bonds, established from its early days, held firm.

The formal structure of the conference was highly inclusive at this stage, as befitted the ambitious worldwide scope envisaged for the projected League. Wilson's own attention and energy were naturally devoted to the implementation of his grand design. Conversely, a common French view was that this was the wrong objective. 'They loathe the League of Nations and say that Wilson's insistence on its being taken first is delaying the Peace', Nicolson noted on 10 February (though himself professing a more indulgent view) (Nicolson 1933, 260). Not until Wilson returned from a month's visit to Washington in the middle of March was he ready to focus on an agenda that, for Lloyd George and Clemenceau, had the issue of reparations and indemnities from Germany as an urgent priority.

What the *Economic Consequences* fails to disclose is that the Council of Four – in effect, the Big Three, after Orlando's marginalisation – only became operational at this point. Wilson is sometimes credited with its inception at the end of March but it seems clear that, even before the President had arrived back, it was House who had made this proposal to Lloyd George, with whom he worked well, and to Clemenceau (Neu 2015, 403). So, on the President's return, it was really Wilson who now stepped into House's shoes, picking up on matters that had been House's province for a month, with an undertow of disgruntlement on either side. Wilson harboured a suspicion that House had sold the pass on some issues, too ready to conciliate Clemenceau and Lloyd George; conversely, both House and the Secretary of State, Robert Lansing, thought that it would have been better if the President had never come to Paris at all. As it was, Wilson had returned from Washington burdened with the necessity of satisfying suspicions in Congress about the scope of this League of Nations of his. Humbled, he now needed concessions on the text of the League's Covenant in order to secure American ratification.

'At the crisis of his fortunes the President was a lonely man', is how the *Economic Consequences* puts it (JMK 2:30). True, far from seeming the master of the whole situation, as he had appeared at the time of his triumphal arrival in Europe in December 1918, Wilson was now publicly somewhat diminished. Privately, too, within the Big Three he was seeking ways to propitiate Lloyd George and Clemenceau on their own agenda, so as to secure their agreement for revision of the Covenant. Keynes does not put this so specifically. All that we read in his third chapter is that 'the most decisive moment in the disintegration of the President's moral position and the clouding of his mind' came when Wilson accepted the argument that pensions and separation allowances qualified as reparations, which is explained as the President's capitulation 'before a masterpiece of the sophist's art' – whatever that meant (JMK 2:33).

The persuasiveness of the *Economic Consequences*, in explaining the final Treaty as a product of the interaction between the Big Three, depends largely upon such eminently quotable parts of its third chapter. The role of Clemenceau, though important, was easiest to understand, as the consistent pursuit of a zero-sum game in which France could only win if Germany lost. But it was the failings of the ostensibly liberal strategies of Lloyd George and, above all, of Wilson that attracted most attention from early readers. In this story, Lloyd George's portrayal was ambivalent, with Keynes's apparent scorn for his defective sense of morality offset against reluctant admiration for his political artistry, especially in manipulating Wilson – perhaps with more comprehensive results than Lloyd George himself had intended. For in the end, of course, 'it was harder to de-bamboozle this old Presbyterian than it had been to bamboozle him; for the former involved his belief in and respect for himself' (JMK 2:34). Here was the sting and the sneer that really hurt, the gibe that was endlessly repeated by Wilson's critics, as though it were a compelling demonstration of the case against him. This satirical vocabulary was not quite so freshly minted as it seemed in 1919. Three years previously Keynes had tried it out in an article referring to German popular support for the war: 'Had the will for peace in Germany been wholehearted and strong and really widespread, it would not have been so easy to bamboozle the people in August 1914. It was necessary to bamboozle them as it was' (JMK 16:183). Now, this tongue-in-cheek term was again pressed into service by the author, this time with an added twist. But did most readers of the *Economic Consequences* really understand what was at stake in this bamboozlement in Chapter 3? And did they fully grasp, by the time they had reached the middle of Chapter 5, some sixty pages later, how it was that Wilson had been duped?

'I cannot here describe', Keynes blandly claims in Chapter 5, 'the endless controversy and intrigue between the Allies themselves, which at last after some months culminated in the presentation to Germany of the reparation chapter in its final form'. Keynes's abstention from further comment at this point is ostensibly justified by a display of general contrition: 'I doubt if anyone who took much part in that debate can look back on it without shame' (JMK 2:95). But the innocent reader will hardly appreciate the extent to which Keynes is engaged, in the paragraphs that follow, on a cover-up of his personal role.

34

For what follows is a discussion of the origin of Article 231 of the Versailles Treaty, the stipulation on which Germany's liability for paying heavy reparations finally came to depend. Of course it is not helpfully headlined 'War Guilt Clause' in the text of the Treaty, but the import is deadly: 'The Allied and Associated governments affirm and Germany accepts the responsibility of Germany and her allies for causing all the loss and damage to which the Allied and Associated governments and their nationals have been subjected as a consequence of the war imposed upon them by the aggression of Germany and her allies'. There is surely no need to establish at length the salience of this issue. In the widely accepted view, pithily stated in the editors' introduction to the proceedings of the international conference commemorating the 75th anniversary of the Treaty: 'At the core of the persistent controversy over the Versailles Treaty lies the question of German war guilt' (Boemeke et al. 1998, 17). By contrast, the *Economic Consequences* simply describes this clause as 'a well and carefully drafted article' (JMK 2:95). But it does not disclose that this careful drafting was largely the work of Dulles, working with none other than Keynes himself.

***

It was not just their professed expertise, however defined, that had brought the two young men together but a largely common political outlook on the big issues. Dulles was more strait-laced than either Keynes or Davis; his Presbyterian background sat more heavily upon him, as did his family connections, notably the distinguished diplomatic career of his maternal grandfather, whose invitation had led this precocious teenage student at Princeton to interrupt his studies in order to assist John Foster in his work as special counsel at the second Hague conference in 1907. Returning to Princeton, Dulles had written a sympathetic paper in defence of pragmatism; he had also developed an admiration for the President of the University, Woodrow Wilson (Guhin 1972, 21–5). It may seem unsurprising that, with the United States' entry in the Great War in 1917, Dulles was to become fully committed to the war aims that he found 'magnificently formulated' by Wilson – whose appointee as Secretary of State, Robert Lansing, was married to Dulles's aunt.

This time it was 'Uncle Bert' who helped persuade his nephew to put his talents at the disposal of the administration and in due course to attend another and even greater international conference (Pruessen 1982, 23ff). It is clear that the connection between the two men remained strong in Paris, giving Dulles more leverage than his comparatively subordinate position might otherwise suggest. And it was the 'Lansing Note' of 5 November 1918 that had canonically defined the terms of the Armistice as agreed with Germany. Virtually everything that the *Economic Consequences* says about the subsequent betrayal of these undertakings in the Treaty derives from the arguments that Dulles consistently put forward during the negotiations, though Keynes only subsequently felt free to acknowledge this explicitly.

The Commission on Reparations had had its first meeting on 3 February 1919. The American members all had some kind of financial expertise, as might be expected. Vance McCormick was a publisher; he was the most obviously political of the members as a Pennsylvania progressive and close to Colonel House. Norman Davis, as we have seen, had made serious money before entering government service, his career closely entangled with that of Thomas Lamont (who later acted as an alternate for Davis) through the J.P. Morgan bank, in ways that were to excite subsequent scandal (Carter 2020, 85–6). Bernard Baruch, the chairman of the Commission, had a long career as a fabulously wealthy Wall Street speculator. Previously Chairman of the War Industries Board, he cultivated a reputation as 'industrial dictator' (which was to be burnished in 1923 by a book about himself that he sponsored to the tune of some $38,000, say half a million dollars at today's values). He was not a man to cross, as Keynes was to discover. Dulles had won the trust of Baruch, for whom he had worked at the War Industries Board, and was himself to serve as a well-rewarded ghostwriter in due course.

Though Baruch and Davis later emerged as prominent public critics of the *Economic Consequences* (while disagreeing with each other on exactly why it merited criticism) the United States delegation had started from a position close to Keynes's own views on reparations – unlike the Commissioners whom Lloyd George had appointed to represent the British Empire. The point was that the latter came fresh from a British postwar general election in which the cry to 'make Germany pay' had often overridden distinctions between open-ended 'indemnities' for the victors, which was a traditional demand, but not sanctioned in the Armistice agreement, and – in a new coinage that had Wilsonian approval – 'reparations' for specific breaches of international law. By conflating the two usages, and instead using such phrases as 'the costs of the war', the scale of what would be demanded from Germany had commonly been described in Britain in highly inflated terms. The sort of figures now in public circulation wildly exceeded any informed estimate of what might be due from Germany as payments to France or Belgium for 'damage done to the civilian population of the Allies and their property', which was the defining language of the Lansing Note.

What Lloyd George had actually done was to ask for advice, not on what was due under the Lansing Note, but instead on Germany's capacity to pay. In the process he had overridden estimates provided by the British Treasury, in which Keynes, as a civil servant with relevant expertise, obviously had had a hand. The Treasury had suggested that it might be possible to exact a sum of around £2 billion within the terms of the Lansing Note. Such a claim did not meet Lloyd George's electioneering needs, so instead he had quickly appointed a committee to report to the Imperial War Cabinet. Acting under acute pressure of time during the closing days of the general election campaign, the committee came up with a wild estimate set as high as £24 billion.

This figure reflected not only the views of its bellicose chairman, the Australian Prime Minister, William Morris Hughes: the scale of the claim was also invested with the authority of another member of the committee, the former Governor of the Bank of England, Lord Cunliffe. There was already bad blood between Keynes and Cunliffe (who had recently sought to have this precocious temporary Treasury official demoted, only to be overruled by Bonar Law, then Chancellor of the Exchequer). But Lloyd George clearly had a soft spot for Cunliffe. In his *War Memoirs* he later recalled that when, in former days, he had once asked the Governor 'how he knew which bills were safe to approve, he replied, "I smell them"' (Lloyd George, *WM* 1:62). This declared reliance on his nose in financial dealings evidently appealed to the Prime Minister's own instincts in 1918.

The immediate outcome was that Lloyd George, in his electioneering, seized on the report that Hughes sent him. The resulting 'indemnity policy' outlined in Lloyd George's speech at Bristol on 11 December is fairly summarised in the *Economic Consequences*: 'First, we have an absolute right to demand the whole cost of the war; second, we propose to demand the whole cost of the war; and third, a committee appointed by direction of the Cabinet believe that it can be done' (JMK 2:90). Along with the eminent judge Lord Sumner, both Cunliffe and the irrepressible Billy Hughes were promptly appointed by Lloyd George, after his election victory, as the three representatives of the British Empire on the Reparations Committee in Paris. The names of neither Sumner nor Cunliffe appear in Keynes's published account, yet their ghostly influence would certainly have been apparent in his story to a well-informed reader such as Dulles. Keynes's derisive soubriquet for them, 'the Heavenly Twins', became well known at the conference, not least to the Americans.

Clearly, then, Keynes's own sympathies were much more with the representatives of the United States than with those of the British Empire when the Reparations Commission began its formal business. The American position was explicitly that the Pre-Armistice Agreement (in effect, the Lansing Note) was binding; but theirs had been the only delegation to make any reference to this agreement in their preliminary statements to the Commission. The French position is pithily expressed by André Tardieu, Clemenceau's chief of staff: 'The Armistice of November 11, 1918, was an unconditional surrender on the part of Germany' (Tardieu 1921, 43).

The form in which the Pre-Armistice Agreement had been drafted between the Allies in late October 1918 had been handled by Wilson's man of business, Colonel House, who was already in Europe, reporting every move to the President in Washington. This process was to come under keen retrospective scrutiny. House's task, aided by a bevy of young assistants, had been to translate Wilson's Fourteen Points into diplomatic language acceptable to all the Allies on the parameters of the peace terms to be negotiated with Germany.

The final text, covered by the Lansing Note, had indeed offered Lloyd George one crucial expansion of the definition of 'reparation' or 'restoration'. These terms had applied in the first instance, and often interchangeably, to the position of Belgium (only later to France) where 'damage done to the civilian population' was obviously as a result of a German invasion that was in itself illegal. But the comparable civilian losses by the British Empire had overwhelmingly been the result of submarine and air activity rather than invasion. Hence the amendment, at British instigation, in the final text of the Lansing Note: 'that compensation will be made by Germany for all damage to the civilian population of the Allies and their property by the aggression of Germany by land, by sea and from the air' (Burnett 1940, 411–12).

The motive for this amendment had been, above all, to include civilian shipping losses. But the use of the more general, open-ended and emotive term 'aggression' was also to prove influential in subsequent arguments. It was Lloyd George's trusted executive assistant, Philip Kerr, who had been responsible for the introduction of the term 'aggression', as he subsequently came to rue with pained surprise (having meanwhile forgotten that the crucial change in the text of the Armistice agreement stood in the archives in his own handwriting) (Gilbert 1966, 31). Keynes clearly appreciated the significance of what had been done here in amending the Lansing Note. He later wrote to Sir Austen Chamberlain, who had succeeded Bonar Law as his political boss at the Treasury and had now read a complimentary copy of the *Economic Consequences*: 'while I agree that much of the Wilsonian code was incapable of strict translation into a treaty, *some* part of it was precise; and in the case of reparations, the formula, over which (in my opinion) we have cheated, was not Wilson's but *our own*' (JMK 17:12, italics in original).

***

Dulles had made it his own too. His address to the Reparations Commission on 13 February 1919 became the classic statement of the American position (and, as will be seen, its text was to be published by Baruch within a year of the publication of the *Economic Consequences*). In effect Dulles's oration was a response to a previous statement of the British Empire case by Hughes, who had sought to extend the scope of Germany's liability for war costs way beyond the Belgian case. Hughes wished to include all the Allies who had taken up arms, as he put it, to right Belgium's wrongs.

The pervasive sense of overriding moral outrage generated here was what Dulles sought to qualify. He did so by making it clear that the relative moderation of the United States' approach to reparations – 'the least drastic in its terms', as he admitted, of those submitted to the Commission – should not be 'misconstrued as indicative of a lack of severity in judgement and in purpose'. On the contrary, 'the American members associate themselves in the most complete and unconditional way with all that has been said in the various memoranda on file relative to the enormity of the crime which Germany has committed' – expressing just as much moral indignation as Hughes, in short (Baruch 1920, 289).

So Dulles had proceeded to ask, 'why, in defiance of these motives, have we proposed reparation in certain limited ways only? It is because, gentlemen, we do not regard ourselves as free'. They did not have 'a blank page upon which we are free to write what we will' (Baruch 1920, 290). In this rhetorically charged way, he directed the commission's attention to 'the agreed basis of peace with Germany', as signed not only by Wilson but by Clemenceau and by Lloyd George too, as well as by Orlando for Italy. 'Gentlemen, we have here an agreement', Dulles continued, shifting from the tone of a moral appeal to the dry specification of a contractual obligation. 'It is an agreement which cannot be ignored, and I am confident that no one here would propose to ignore it' (Baruch 1920, 292). His professed confidence was, of course, misplaced if he thought that Hughes, let alone Cunliffe and Sumner, would be impressed. But Dulles kept reiterating that it was too late to change a bargain that had already been struck – the time for argument had been 'in the early days of November, 1918, and not today' (Baruch 1920, 294). The Lansing Note was thus the master text. And it was, of course, a legal text. 'It is not enough that an act be immoral, that it be cruel, that it be unjust, unless at the same time it be illegal' (Baruch 1920, 295).

Likewise, complete repayment *to Belgium* of all war costs was thus justified, because of German violation of an international covenant on Belgian neutrality. Dulles's reasoning here, as we can now readily confirm from contemporary documentation of House's negotiations, followed the so-called Lippmann–Cobb memorandum of 29 October 1918. Primarily the work of Walter Lippmann, another of the young progressives seconded to government service in Paris, the nub of the argument on Belgium was the generally acknowledged illegality of Germany's violation of the 1839 and 1870 Treaties guaranteeing its independence. 'The initial act of invasion was illegitimate and therefore all the consequences of that act are of the same character. Among the consequences may be put the war debt of Belgium' (PWW 51:500). Now the *Economic Consequences* did not actually endorse this conclusion, since its validity 'could only be on the ground of the breach of international law involved in the invasion of Belgium' – whereas the Fourteen Points had failed to invoke such a claim, thus leaving it outside the terms of the Lansing Note (JMK 2:74). For Keynes, it was only when the Belgian provision had been accepted by the German representatives that it became a valid claim.

'It is a popular delusion', the *Economic Consequences* comments, 'to think of Belgium as the principal victim of the war' (JMK 2:79). Perhaps this suggests, in emotional response as well as in legal argument, at least a hairline crack between how Keynes and Dulles understood the position. The Lippmann–Cobb memorandum, as House was later at pains to put on record, had been circulated to all the Allies in signing up to the Lansing Note. It was this, in the American view, that established the uniqueness of Belgium alone in its entitlement to recover war costs because of the acknowledged breach of international law. 'The illegality of this act and the duty of making reparation have already been formally admitted by Germany', Dulles concluded in seeking to make his case watertight (Baruch 1920, 295). For that too went back to the Lansing Note, in sealing a contract duly accepted by both sides.

Hughes's response, clearly reinforced by advice from Sumner, made some legalistic points on international law; but its more effective appeal was to moral intuition. Hughes sought to build on the undisputed point that Germany was at fault in its violation of international law over Belgium: 'Great Britain and France were *bound* to defend it; the United States and Italy were *entitled* to defend it' (Baruch 1920, 302). His argument gestured towards an issue that Dulles had ignored in his analysis: whether the *enforcement* of international law depended on a (moral) decision to intervene by other, disinterested countries. In an era when the status of an international court or other body with authority to act was unclear, this was surely a relevant point. Hughes's contention was that all the costs of an unjust war should be borne by the aggressor: a proposition that he sought to sustain by citing Wilson himself on the reign of law. Dulles's appeal to 'contract', on this reading, was thus all too narrowly framed. 'We claim no penalty, but reparation only,' Hughes concluded. 'We ask for justice, not revenge' (Baruch 1920, 312). Here, too, the argument shifted unsteadily between moral and legal criteria.

44

The Reparation Commission was clearly deadlocked. Dulles made a further formal submission on 19 February. He now sought to clarify the only two ways in which Germany could be held accountable:

> that *by agreement* Germany is liable to make compensation for all damage done to the civilian population of the Allies and their property by the aggression of Germany by land, by sea, and from the air; that *by operation of law* those who have been the victim of admittedly illegal acts, such as the violation of Belgium, the torpedoing of merchant vessels without warning, the inhumane treatment of prisoners of war, etc, etc, are entitled to reparation. (Baruch 1920, 324–5, italics in original)

Thus either contract or international law was necessary to make Germany liable. Though Dulles did not mention this, perhaps in the case of Belgium it was the acceptance of the Lippmann–Cobb memorandum by the Allies that empowered them to enforce the operation of law through the terms of the projected peace treaty. Indeed Dulles's argument seems repeatedly to stumble on this point, with some haziness about where a moral obligation shades into a legal requirement, with important implications for how we understand the concept of 'war guilt'. Did it simply entail liability for a legally enforceable debt or did it impute a moral judgement?

In face of French doubts about the status of the Pre-Armistice Agreement itself, Dulles reaffirmed his earlier position: 'We find every element legally necessary to constitute a binding contract' (Baruch 1920, 327). Moreover, in conclusion, Dulles scorned Hughes's suggestion that the violation of a Treaty intended to benefit Belgium could confer compensating benefits on those who had acted in Belgium's defence – in effect that the British Empire should be compensated for doing its duty, like a policeman. It was international law that made Germany's invasion illegal, hence 'Belgium stands in a special position by reason of Germany's breach of her covenant not to make war on Belgium,' as Germany now accepted (Baruch 1920, 334). But any German liability for the general costs of the war would have to depend on some explicit agreement. So, faced with intractable conflicts of opinion, Dulles acknowledged an impasse within the Commission on the point over which they had differed: 'Our debate has revolved around the meaning of the declaration of November 4, 1918' (Baruch 1920, 336).

Once more, then, the true import of the Lansing Note (including the indictment, inserted at the behest of the British, of 'the aggression of Germany by land, by sea and from the air') emerged as crucial. Moreover, it did so at a moment when Dulles's suggestion of going back to the four men who had agreed to its terms proved impracticable. For in late February 1919 Lloyd George was temporarily back in London, trying to settle labour disputes; Clemenceau was in Paris, but convalescent after an assassination attempt; and Wilson, having painstakingly obtained agreement in Paris on a Covenant for the League of Nations, was on shipboard taking this draft back for approval in Washington, DC. John Foster Dulles thus had to rely on his Uncle Bert to salvage the situation by sending the President, now aboard the USS *George Washington*, a telegram that was signed also by Baruch, Davis and McCormick as Commissioners plus, of course, House, now acting head of the US delegation.

Their telegram rehearsed the position taken up by the United States, specifically in the Lansing Note; it updated Wilson on the impasse in the Reparations Commission; and it appealed for clarification. Their dilemma was now clear. Although they did not relish 'appearing to be bound to legal technicalities', they told Wilson that any move to include war costs in the treaty 'opens the way to a complete departure from the agreed terms of peace based on your 14 points and subsequent addresses'. The political situation in the Allied countries, it was acknowledged, 'will make it most difficult for their delegates to take any attitude other than insistence upon the complete reparation which they have promised their people and which all our inquiries show the people of the Allied countries feel to be just and due to them' (PWW 55:211). So there was a real and acute dilemma here.

In the circumstances, Wilson's response was robust. In a telegram of three sentences, sent from the *George Washington* on 23 February 1919, the President first told Lansing that they were 'bound in honor' not to include war costs and, secondly, offered this sharp reproof: 'The time to think of this was before the conditions of peace were communicated to the enemy unconditionally'. Finally, in terms that would similarly be echoed in the *Economic Consequences*, Wilson declared that their dissent on the war costs claim should be based 'not on the ground of the intrinsic injustice of it but on the ground that it is clearly inconsistent with what we deliberately led the enemy to expect and can not now honorably alter simply because we have the power' (PWW 55:231).

It seemed as though, free of the immediate atmosphere of Paris, Wilson had recovered his voice as the prophet of a just and honourable peace, just as Dulles and Keynes had always hoped. Conversely, once Wilson had returned to Paris in the middle of March 1919, his status almost immediately declined to that of a politician anxious to square the political circle on a number of outstanding issues, of which the vexed question of reparations was only one. After all, his highly inconvenient trip back and forth across the ocean to Washington – thus taking him away from the conference for nearly a month – was not because of the deadlock over reparations but because of an issue that stood even higher in the President's own concerns: the fate of his proposals for a League of Nations. Reparations could wait. Yet here was the issue that was to dominate the reception of the Treaty, not least in the *Economic Consequences*. And reparations, of course, were justified in the Treaty by the 'War Guilt Clause', on which the *Economic Consequences* was largely silent – for reasons that require further exploration.

2

What Really Happened at Paris?
The War Guilt Clause

The sequence of events in Paris over the reparations issue has long been made clear through the work of scholars working from the massive documentation that later became available, piece by piece, from both governmental and private archives. Some of this initially came in direct response to the *Economic Consequences*. Within two months of its publication, Dulles had a long letter published in *The Times* in February 1920, making two linked disclosures. One was to reveal – or confirm – that there had indeed been dissent among Wilson's advisors over the legitimacy of including war costs, specifically over pensions and separations allowances, in what was chargeable to Germany. The other revelation was that the crucial argument for doing this had come from Smuts, whose name, like those of the Heavenly Twins or indeed Dulles himself, had not appeared in the *Economic Consequences*.

Keynes immediately replied in a letter to *The Times*, declaring his own 'sympathy, when I was in Paris, with Mr Dulles's sustained and eloquent struggle to ensure a peace which should be in accordance with the engagements of his country and of mine' (JMK 17:26). Dulles privately thanked Keynes, who then replied to Dulles in the same vein on 2 March 1920: 'I fancy we agree pretty much at heart about what happened in Paris, and only differ as to the tactics and procedure of the immediate future' (JMK 17:31–2). Both things – the Anglo-American agreement and the difference – were substantially true, and were soon to be advertised more fully. The context should be remembered: notably that by this point President Wilson was a desperately sick man, clinging on in the White House to the notion that the Treaty could pass through Congress unamended, an inflexible stand that had helped force Lansing's recent resignation, with defeat in the Senate now impending. Dulles, caught in an awkward clash of loyalties, emerged as the spokesman for the official American position as it had been asserted in Paris a year previously, in more optimistic times, alternately corroborating and challenging what Keynes had published.

'I, too, wrote a book, *The Making of the Reparation and Economic Sections of the Treaty*', Baruch was to assert in his memoirs, making clear his own subsequent disdain for the author of the *Economic Consequences*. 'There is no questioning the brilliance and originality of some of his thoughts; but not even Keynesian theory can repeal the fundamental laws of economics' (Baruch 1960, 121). Such comments are drenched in retrospective bile, of course, but even in 1921 the book issued in Baruch's name responded to 'much misconception' and 'many misstatements of fact' in circulation about the parts of the Treaty dealing with reparations, with Keynes an obvious target. Baruch claimed to write on behalf of his colleagues in the US delegation – not least their legal advisor, and indeed the book's true authorship rested largely with Dulles. Its import was serious and recognised as such on both sides of the Atlantic by those intent on pursuing the true story.

Dulles's debate with Hughes about the principles at stake was now reprinted in Baruch's lengthy addenda (from which I have quoted above). There was also the revelation of Wilson's endorsement of Dulles's position in his telegram from the *George Washington*, which Keynes called 'a new historical fact of high importance'. A further document was the actual text that had swayed Wilson on pensions – what Keynes now acidly termed 'a secret memorandum prepared by General Smuts for the four heads of state, which Mr Baruch feels himself at liberty to print in full' (JMK 3:93–4).

Other publications followed: first *What Really Happened at Paris*, edited by House and Seymour in 1921, and subsequently their four-volume edition of selections from House's diary. The disclosures that Keynes himself had made public at the end of 1919 were thus seized upon by others, sometimes in support and sometimes in reproof, with an incremental flow of further documentation. In the process, the sense of Anglo-American affinity at the level of the younger officials in Paris was breached by an emerging fracture line, sometimes as wide as the Atlantic.

Keynes had been warned, in advance of publishing his *Economic Consequences*, of what to expect by Arthur Salter, a perceptive civil servant then serving as General Secretary of the Reparations Commission. 'I think there are two things in the book (neither of them touching its main theme) which are likely to do a great deal of harm', Salter had written in October 1919, having seen a proof copy. Citing his own experience in working closely with Americans, Salter warned Keynes that 'in anything like diplomacy, they think we're too clever for them'. In which case, 'the presentation of the Peace negotiations as essentially the outmanoeuvring of a simple-minded "Presbyterian preacher" by two cunning diplomatists will have a very disastrous effect'. It would naturally be exploited by Wilson's political opponents. And secondly, so Salter cautioned, not only was the President's own vanity at stake: his liberal supporters would feel affronted, not least in the context of Wilson's debilitating illness (JMK 17:5–6). All of this came to pass. Whereas in Britain the *Economic Consequences* was seized upon by the liberal left to indict Lloyd George, in the United States its message and tone alike provoked indignant dissent from liberals who felt a stubborn loyalty towards their embattled hero in his doomed struggle over Congressional ratification of the Treaty and the League of Nations.

And all of this also affected how the story of the Treaty negotiations over reparations was received throughout the inter-war period. From an American perspective, the massive two volumes eventually published by the Columbia University Press in 1940, meticulously edited by Philip Mason Burnett, stand as a landmark. The work's full title is significant: *Reparation at the Paris Peace Conference – from the Standpoint of the American Delegation*. This is what it claimed to reveal; this is what Burnett duly delivered, both in publishing a wide range of documents and in supplying a meticulous exegesis, which has rarely been challenged. It was stressed that these were only the American documents; and obviously in 1940 both the French and the British had more pressing matters to attend to. Nonetheless it is primarily this collection, and its interpretation by Burnett, that has rightly held the field in subsequent understanding of how the reparations issue was settled in Paris.

What is particularly relevant here is not only the import but the provenance of this archival source. The fact that the two volumes were prefaced with a foreword by John Foster Dulles is significant. It was his small mountain of documents, brought home from Paris, that duly became, for Burnett, 'the foundation of the documentary section of this book' (Burnett 1940, 1:xix). Some of the official material is now replicated in other published scholarly editions, notably the relevant volumes of the Wilson Papers; but Burnett had privileged access to important documents drafted by Dulles himself, especially his own records of informal meetings of the 'experts' on reparations (Burnett 1940, 1:158). The preface that Dulles contributed to these two volumes explicitly commends the efforts of his old colleagues McCormick, Baruch, Lamont and Davis on reparations: 'These four functioned in complete harmony and constituted a highly effective unit' (Burnett 1940, 1:vii). Implicitly, Dulles was the fifth man, now belatedly presenting his case, just as the *Economic Consequences* had precipitately presented Keynes's case.

∗∗∗

The Dulles version, judiciously summarised in Burnett's pages, does not explicitly challenge the Keynes version but it certainly fills some gaps. Dulles's clashes with Hughes in the Reparations Commission about the legitimacy of war costs are given due prominence; but so is the implication that arose for the percentage distribution of any payments by Germany as between different recipients. It was Dulles, in the middle of February 1919, who had seized on the fact that, while it would obviously be in the interests of the

British Empire, by including war costs, to increase its share of the proceeds (and thus also to inflate the total bill), this manoeuvre came at a price. For it would – proportionately or in percentage terms – come at the expense of the reparations actually available for civilian damage to France or Belgium.

This conflict over percentages henceforth became a pivotal issue. Dulles's thinking went further, accommodating to the possibility that, though he may have technically won the argument with Hughes over any legal or contractual liability for Germany to pay war costs, the political reality was otherwise. The Americans might, after all, have to agree with the British Empire that Germany should nonetheless be held responsible in some way – theoretically if not financially – for going to war in the first place. In which case, as the 'Dulles drafts' had already begun suggesting during February 1919, an acceptance of moral or 'theoretical' liability might well be due from Germany, thus fulfilling the popular expectations aroused by Allied leaders like Lloyd George and Clemenceau, not to mention Hughes. After all, the moral condemnation of German aggression had become commonplace, not least in transatlantic liberal incantations over the origins of the war. Here was the way forward, once Wilson (from the *George Washington* in late February) had explicitly ruled out war costs as a contractual requirement under the Lansing Note.

It was at this point that Dulles became tireless in suggesting how the circle might be squared. His own drafts suggested that, since reparations would in practice be fixed by the Germans' capacity to pay, their actual liability could be limited either by naming a fixed sum or, if that were not possible, by specifying a time limit after which payments would cease.

And it was along these lines that the Big Three, in Wilson's absence overseas, had determined to move in seizing the initiative. On 10 March they appointed one expert each to confer about reparations, justifiably described by Burnett as 'the first official step in taking the reparation question away from the big Commission; in getting it – confidentially – into the hands of the British, the French, and the Americans' (Burnett 1940, 1:53). The American expert chosen to serve was Norman Davis; Clemenceau delegated this task (along with most other reparations issues) to his colleague Louis Loucheur; and the British likewise nominated a politician, Edwin Montagu.

Montagu was in the British Cabinet as Secretary of State for India, but he worked in Paris with a wider brief on the reparations issue, on which he was a dove rather than a hawk. Lloyd George had made no secret of this. For example at a meeting of the Council of Four in late March, Wilson referred one proposal about reparations for expert advice: 'I asked Messrs Baruch, Davis, and Lamont to study this text and they should get together with your specialists'. Lloyd George responded: 'I will put them in touch with Mr Montague [sic], who has a more flexible mind than Lord Sumner and who is above all accustomed to looking at problems from the political angle' (PWW 56:448–9). Montagu was thus a Liberal in more than name only; moreover he was an old Cambridge friend and patron of Keynes, who now, as a civil servant, reported to him in Paris as his responsible minister. When Montagu was absent in England, it was Keynes who stood in for him (alongside Sumner) at a meeting on 18 March. The Americans soon made a joke to the effect that when Lloyd George was taking a hard line he brought Sumner and Cunliffe, the 'Heavenly

Twins', to the meetings; but when he sought conciliation he nominated Keynes and Montagu.

The newly constituted Council of Four had indeed come into the picture at this point, following the President's return. We therefore have the indefatigable Mantoux's notes of its meeting on 24 March, which capture Wilson's sense that 'we should take in hand the most difficult and urgent questions among the four of us, questions such as reparations', a proposal on which he had found ready support. 'Our experts will never come to an agreement', said Lloyd George. 'The problem is two-fold: we must know what the Germans will be able to pay, and how we will distribute it among ourselves' (PWW 56:208–9).

In saying this, Lloyd George was drawing on the conclusions of a conclave of his close advisors, held at Fontainebleau, which had produced an ostensibly high-minded memorandum on the principles that should inform a lasting peace. In this endeavour, winning consent from Germany was crucial since:

> [I]n the end if she feels that she has been unjustly treated
> in the peace of 1919 she will find means of exacting
> retribution from her conquerors. The impression, the
> deep impression, made upon the human heart by four
> years of unexampled slaughter will disappear with the
> hearts upon which it has been marked by the terrible
> sword of the great war. (Lloyd George, TPT 405)

This is close to the general perspective of the *Economic Consequences*, of course; but the real question is how the rhetoric was translated into policy. The British now suggested a permanent Reparation Commission, and proposed that, given that the amount due in reparation would exceed what Germany was capable of paying, an annual sum should be required, with the number of years it was payable limited to the generation that had made the war – say, thirty years.

This was much as Dulles had already suggested; but on percentages, the British Empire proposal inverted his reasoning. Dulles, as we have seen, had hoped to use percentages to persuade the French against the inclusion of war costs since these would, by inflating the total amount demanded, necessarily deflate the percentage due to France of whatever sum was eventually extracted from Germany. The British instead proposed to fix the percentages due, year by year, so that whatever amount was distributed annually would be divided, with France assigned 50 per cent and the British Empire 30 per cent.

Clearly, with war costs excluded, it would be difficult for the countries of the Empire to find sufficient categories of actual reparations to get up to their notional 30 per cent quota. The physical damage was on the ground in France and Belgium; the British Empire's costs were disproportionately in pensions. Hitherto, of course, war pensions and separation allowances had constituted part of a claim for the payment of an indemnity covering the full costs of the war; but now that there was no further talk of 'indemnities' after Wilson's edict from the *George Washington*, the question of whether pensions were better considered as 'reparations' obviously arose.

The key to the outcome lay in the interaction between the American and British delegations in redefining the scope of reparations after Fontainebleau. And in this task, the experts on both sides were naturally active in producing the specific solutions that were then duly passed up for the approval of the Big Three. On the American side, then, the important figures were Baruch, McCormick and Davis, sometimes Lamont too, and with Dulles in attendance as necessary whenever policy decisions had to be translated into a legally tight text. On the British side, Lloyd George exercised his own discretion over whom to choose as the bearers of his (sometimes conflicting) messages; thus he sent not only Keynes but also Sumner and Cunliffe to the series of fraught meetings that took place from 25 to 28 March.

On 28 March, as we can see from Mantoux's notes of the Council of Four, Keynes was introduced by Lloyd George to speak to a new proposal that the experts now had before them. 'Our uncertainty chiefly concerned Germany's capacity to pay', Keynes explained. 'We proposed to tell the Germans: "Here is what you owe; but we have not yet determined how much you are able to pay." It is this second point that we will have to discuss with them' (PWW 56:357). Such discussion would presumably have been intended for the projected plenary negotiations with Germany at Versailles, once the Allied conference in Paris had determined its own agreed position on what to offer.

Keynes found a sympathetic hearer in Wilson for adopting this approach – rather than, as it appeared to Wilson, adopting the French demand for 'a blank check' from Germany. Hence the President's approving comment: 'Mr Keynes's proposal was very much different' (PWW 56:357–8). Maybe it was; but while Keynes might have wished to focus on how much the Germans were able to pay, what he meant by telling them 'what you owe' was altogether more ambiguous. Would they owe an actual contractual debt? Or was this a purely theoretical obligation, set on some higher plane of morality? There was indeed much to debate here.

In retrospect, Dulles offered a pertinent remark when he observed: 'The Conference was one on the "Conditions of Peace"; there was, properly speaking, no "Peace Conference"' (Burnett 1940, 1:ix). As the chapter entitled 'The Conference' in the *Economic Consequences* had explained at the start, the French were not alone in anticipating 'a double process of compromise, first of all to suit the ideas of their allies and associates, and secondly in the course of the peace conference proper with the Germans themselves' (JMK 2:17). So at the moment when the reparations clauses were agreed, the assumption was still that the German viewpoint would receive serious consideration, with the possibility of changes.

Instead, Clemenceau was to insist on simply presenting the Allied draft of the Treaty to Germany on a take-it-or-leave-it basis. This was what eventually happened on the fateful day, 7 May 1919, with Count Brockdorff-Rantzau leading a German delegation that ultimately had little real alternative but to sign. As Dulles later put it: 'Thus what was originally conceived of as a basis of discussion became without discussion the Treaty terms' (Burnett 1940, 1:ix). These terms were never, in practice, subject to the processes of negotiation implicit in the Armistice agreement of November 1918. If not only Clemenceau but also Lloyd George was to change his stance over the status of the Paris conference, it was surely because the British Prime Minister had meanwhile appeared before the electorate in triumph as 'the man who won the war', not as the man who proposed to negotiate with the Germans on equal terms. The difference was that, unlike Clemenceau, Lloyd George also eventually acknowledged his bondage to the Lansing Note.

At any rate, in late March 1919 it seems to have been generally accepted, by the Big Three and their henchmen alike, that the notional amount 'owed' by Germany was part of the smoke and mirrors in this performance; whereas pulling an actual rabbit out of an actual hat, in the form of actual payments from Germany, would be a matter of practical feasibility. If Clemenceau was casting around for some way to get Germany to pay more in aggregate, the problem for Lloyd George was now different: to secure a large enough share of the spoils for the British Empire under the requisite definition of what qualified as reparations. It was in this context that the proposal for pensions and separation allowances to be regarded as 'reparations' became crucial.

***

In the *Economic Consequences*, Keynes remained evasively obscure about the drafting of the War Guilt Clause in the Treaty. He wrote that it was 'only a matter of words, of virtuosity in draftsmanship, which does no one any harm, and which probably seemed much more important at the time than it ever will again between now and judgement day' (JMK 2:96). Keynes's gross misrepresentation of the effect, obviously misguided even by the time he drafted his book in the late summer of 1919, is followed by five pages explaining how German liability for Allied war pensions, hitherto thought of as war costs or indemnities and thus inadmissible, were redefined as reparations. This extension was transparently engineered so as to boost the proportion received by countries of the British Empire – setting Australian war pensioners alongside French farmers as recipients – but its consequential effect was likewise obvious in tripling the total amount demanded from Germany. Admittedly, there was a proposal for a thirty-year time limit to offset the total impact on Germany's liability; but, when this stipulation fell by the wayside, as we shall see, the effect was indeed to triple the extent of the total reparations claim upon Germany under Article 231.

What was at stake in making this move? 'The point is whether it was covered by the Lansing Note, which was an interpretation of the Fourteen Points insisted upon by the Allies and conveyed by the American Government to the Germans before the Armistice was signed', so Lloyd George later acknowledged. 'Did the pension claim go beyond the Lansing clause?' (Lloyd George, *TPT* 492). If this sounds like a rather lawyerly way of putting the issue, it should be remembered that, as Lloyd George stated prominently in the preface to his two-volume work *The Truth About the Peace Treaties* in 1938, he had himself been a practising lawyer and 'with that experience in my memory, I have chosen the material at my disposal for the book' (Lloyd George, *TPT* 5). His book duly cites the argument that Sumner had formally presented on 30 March 1919, notably his reassurance that no real conflict arose over what could be claimed: 'The truth is that much "reparation damage" might be described as part of the "costs of the war" to the country concerned' (Lloyd George *TPT* 494).

The fact was, however, that the President had remained unpersuaded by this style of argument from Sumner. It was not until the following two days that the highly significant shift in the Allied position on pensions was achieved on the advice of Smuts: much to his subsequent chagrin. It was Smuts, moreover, who later privately encouraged Keynes, on his resignation in June 1919, 'to set about writing a clear connected account of what the financial and economic clauses of the treaty actually are and mean, and what their probable results will be' (JMK 17:3). The fact that such inspiration for Keynes's tract came from Smuts is not, of course, acknowledged in the *Economic Consequences*, which omits his name altogether. It is easy to see why; it suited both men at the time not to reveal their roles here; and Keynes might even be commended for his chivalry in not reproaching a friend and an ally.

Only with the publication of Keynes's far less prominent sequel in 1922, *A Revision of the Treaty*, did he supply a more candid version of the crucial episode. He now explicitly cited Smuts's memorandum on pensions of 31 March 1919, of which Baruch's book had meanwhile published a full copy (Baruch 1920, 29–32). Moreover, Keynes was able to quote a graphic eye-witness description of its effect upon President Wilson; this was taken from a lecture that Thomas Lamont had given, meanwhile published in the collection *What Really Happened at Paris* (1920). The punchline was the President's reaction to the unanimous advice of the American advisors that Smuts's proposal defied all logic. 'Logic! Logic!', exclaimed the President, 'I don't care a damn for logic. I am going to include pensions!' (House and Seymour 1921, 272). With this revelation thus in print, Keynes now claimed in his *Revision of the Treaty* that it justified him to 'set forth, for the inspection of Englishmen and our Allies, the moral basis on which two-thirds of our claims against Germany rest' (JMK 3:104).

All of this may suggest that Wilson and Smuts each made what they considered a prudent, realistic political decision to compromise on this issue, perhaps to save the Treaty and the League of Nations alike. True, Smuts's advocacy proved uniquely influential with the President precisely because Smuts was so highly esteemed in liberal circles. But it is also surely significant how the old soldier had gone about mounting his argument. The Smuts memorandum opened by stating: 'The extent to which reparation can be claimed from Germany depends in the main on the meaning of the last reservation made by the Allies in their Note to President Wilson, November 1918. That reservation was agreed to by President Wilson and accepted by the German Government in the Armistice negotiations'. Smuts then quoted the relevant paragraph from the Lansing Note (Hancock and van der Poel 1966, 4:96). Lloyd George had meanwhile overruled Sumner (and also the French) in their wish to set aside the Lansing Note. So yet again, in reading what Smuts had written, Wilson was faced – just as he had been when aboard the *George Washington* – with the challenge of interpreting his own intentions as declared to the world in November 1918; but he now had Smuts's expansive 'commonsense construction' of its implications before him.

The sequence of events was dramatic, indeed frenetic. On the morning of 1 April 1919 there was a meeting of the experts, with Montagu and Keynes charged with the uncongenial task of telling the Americans that Lloyd George insisted on including pensions. But this was no longer, of course, mounted as a challenge to the status of the Lansing Note but as a reinterpretation. It seems that not only the three US Commissioners (Baruch, McCormick and Davis) but also Lamont and Dulles conferred with Colonel House, and then all had lunch together before the crucial meeting of the President and his advisors at 2 p.m. the same day.

Dulles left his own memorandum of this encounter. 'The President was first shown the reparation plan which had been agreed to the previous day with Messrs Montague [sic] and Keynes', Dulles noted, explaining this as 'a scheme to avoid a present decision by the American Commissioners on the propriety of including pensions and separation allowances'. But Keynes and Montagu had now been countermanded by Lloyd George; and meanwhile Wilson had seen Smuts's memorandum, and been very much impressed by it. Dulles records that the President evidently ruminated on its import: 'that he did not regard this as a matter of decision on strict legal principles; that it was probable that the question of pensions was not specifically considered in November'. On the *George Washington* six weeks previously, of course, the President's retort was that November had been explicitly the moment to think of such points. But now, instead, Wilson claimed that he was 'continuously finding new meanings and the necessity of broad application of principles previously enunciated even though imperfectly', which Dulles evidently found hard to take. He put it to Wilson that the Smuts analysis was hardly logical in its categorisation of ex-soldiers as civilians. It was in this context, then, that the President had stated that 'he did not feel bound by considerations of logic' in deciding otherwise (PWW 56:498–9).

It was indeed a telling moment when Wilson made this political decision to reject the unanimous advice of his own experts, who were clearly shaken. Dulles's record naturally focussed on the legal point at issue. It was McCormick who noted the political implications for Britain and France – 'because both Prime Ministers believe their government will be overthrown if the facts are known' – and he also recorded: 'We went to our office after our talk with the President to meet Montague [*sic*] and Keynes of the British Delegation' (PWW 56:501). These rueful British experts had likewise been overruled by their own boss, of course, and they were now to be closeted with the dejected Americans over the next couple of days in picking up the pieces. Throughout 1 and 2 April it was Montagu and Keynes who negotiated for the British, on the second day with Sumner in addition. The three US Commissioners (Baruch, McCormick and Davis) were again reinforced by the presence of Dulles.

Dulles was certainly needed because the legal implications of what had been done were crucial, given the American insistence on the contractual implications of the Lansing Note, as Dulles kept pointing out. As a result, he now developed an 'oblique' form of words that asserted German responsibility for the war, with all its consequential loss and damage. Keynes made a few recorded interventions but left most of the talking to Montagu, his ministerial boss. It was through them that the American drafts were conveyed to Lloyd George and on that basis the Council of Four considered the issue at another important meeting on 5 April, from which the text of Articles 231 and 232 was to emerge, finalised a couple of days later.

Little wonder, then, that the *Economic Consequences* adopts such a commanding – virtually proprietorial – tone in elucidating these texts. Keynes's point is that, in Article 231, 'the President could read it as [a] statement of admission on Germany's part of *moral* responsibility for bringing about the war, while the Prime Minister could explain it as an admission of financial liability for the general costs of the war' (JMK 2:95–6). The notes of Hankey and Mantoux confirm that it was Keynes himself (along with Lamont and Loucheur) who was to take to the Council of Four the revised final text of this clause, adding the requirement that 'the Enemy States accept' the claims made, which was wording that had dropped out of an earlier draft (PWW 57:79).

The *Economic Consequences* likewise puts its own gloss on Article 232, covering Germany's actual resources: 'the Prime Minister could point out that in the context it emphasises to the reader the assumption of Germany's theoretic liability asserted in the preceding Article'. This description of the liability as 'theoretic', echoing the terminology that Dulles had privately been employing since mid-February, may have puzzled some readers but it surely confirms the insider status of Keynes's account here. And so, of course, does his further exegesis of the wording about 'aggression' – originally Philip Kerr's of course – which 'being practically a quotation from the pre-armistice conditions, satisfied the scruples of the President' (JMK 2:96). All of this was consistent, not only with Dulles's familiar appeals to the Lansing Note, but also with his prior development of a category of 'theoretical liability'.

It was the drafts of these Articles that formed the agenda of the Council of Four meeting on 5 April, held as usual at Wilson's Paris residence. But the President himself was now ill in bed; House substituted for him, reporting back frequently to Wilson's sickroom, and was supported by Davis. Both Mantoux and Hankey were in attendance so we have full notes of what was said. Lloyd George supported the French in saying that the draft of Article 231 'is insufficient to permit us to face the political difficulties which we can expect from both British and French opinion' (PWW 57:6). Mantoux records Davis's comment: 'It is not the American delegation which wanted to introduce that sentence into the text'. This riposte from Keynes's closest American friend was surely well-informed in its hint that there had been another hand in the drafting as well as that of Dulles – whose own position Davis now faithfully echoed: 'We can write that Germany is morally responsible for the war and for all its consequences and that, legally, she is responsible for damages to property and persons, according to the formula adopted'. House then intervened, as the guardian of the Lansing Note: 'We must not draft this text in such a way that it appears to violate our own commitments'. At which point, Clemenceau pounced: 'It is a question of wording; I believe we can find a way out' (PWW 57:8).

It was what happened next that upset Davis, leading him to think that House was poorly prepared on the matter. For it was also at this meeting that the stipulation of a thirty-year fixed period for the payment of reparations was removed. Lord Sumner claimed that the thirty-year term had been inserted by Montagu, in the belief that this had been the wish of Lloyd George, who now made it clear in person that this was not so (or was no longer so). As the discussion went to and fro, House became restive, interjecting at one point that 'a few minutes ago agreement had appeared imminent. President Wilson had always understood that the estimate was to be based on what Germany could pay in a period of 30 years'. After Lloyd George again indicated dissent, Davis made his most forthright declaration: 'President Wilson had understood that by including pensions, the total amount was not increased, owing to the 30 years limit, but that their inclusion only formed a more equitable basis for distribution' (PWW 57:16).

Davis spoke as an advisor; House spoke with an authority delegated to him from the ailing President himself. House thus ended the session by simply proposing that nothing should be said about the thirty-year limit. This was duly omitted and, with its sudden disappearance, the inclusion of war pensions indeed tripled the actual amount of reparations demanded from Germany in the Treaty as presented to the Germans, prefaced with the War Guilt Clause as Article 231.

***

This was not what the US delegation had wanted. They had been overruled by Wilson on the inclusion of pensions; they had been let down by House on the thirty-year safety net. If anyone had been bamboozled, it was Colonel House, of whom Lloyd George wrote in retrospect: 'It is perhaps to his credit that he was not nearly as cunning as he thought he was' (Lloyd George TPT 246).

Davis later persisted in the contention that, even with no thirty-year limit, the amount of reparations actually payable by Germany would have been limited by a potential American

veto over the issue of bonds. He engaged in a public controversy with his formerly close friend Keynes on this issue. On
this point Dulles could not accept Davis's interpretation, so
there was no united American position; indeed Dulles was
now drifting back into agreement with Keynes on the unwisdom of demanding 'paper debts' (Pruessen 1982, 82).

Baruch's suspicion of Keynes was more intractable.
In private he was still warning American negotiators during the Second World War: 'Look out for this fellow, he is a
double crosser' (Moggridge 1992, 743). But in public Baruch's
difference with the *Economic Consequences*, as he stated it
at the time, was based on a broader judgement on Wilson's
strategy as one of realism: 'The Treaty may not embrace all
he desired, but I believe that it embodies all that could have
been obtained' (Baruch 1920, 8). After all, the exact provisions
on reparations could always be amended in future, as indeed
they were in 1921; but the problem was not so much one of
debt as one of guilt. Keynes continued to insist that only more
fundamental and formal revision would meet the needs of a
situation in which Germany felt wronged.

The question remains, why had Dulles been so insis-
tent on adding a War Guilt Clause? We need to remember
that he had brought it up in the first place precisely because of
his argument that pensions were *not* covered by the contract
stipulated in the Lansing Note. In which case, there was no
way that pensions could be legally due for reimbursement by
Germany except with the cover of a new and separate provision, inserted at this late stage into the Treaty itself. With his
rather blinkered legalistic view of the matter, Article 231 was
simply a matter of clever drafting to patch up the contract

retrospectively; and this reasoning was implicitly adopted by Keynes in the *Economic Consequences*. Yet as soon as the draft Treaty was presented to the Germans in May 1919, the issue of war guilt was seized upon, not as a technical legal provision, but as a burning issue of moral responsibility and guilt. 'We are required to admit that we alone are war-guilty', Count Brockdorff-Rantzau was the first to declare but, of course, by no means the last (Lloyd George, *TPT* 678).

Here was an irremediable lapse of judgement, as Dulles himself came to recognise, certainly by the time that Burnett's edition was published. 'Analysis of the documents shows that the participants suffered from "blind spots"', Dulles now wrote. 'Of these the most important is that illustrated by the "war guilt" provision (Article 231). In the light of subsequent developments it may be that this article was the most important single article in the Treaty' (Burnett 1940, 1:xi). This was a handsome acknowledgement to offer by way of apology.

How far Keynes had recognised the point is less easy to document. When his *Revision of the Treaty* was published in 1922 it contained one passage that ought to have made uncomfortable reading. 'It has not been understood in England or America how deep a wound has been inflicted on Germany's self-respect by compelling her, not merely to perform acts, but to subscribe to beliefs which she did not in fact accept', the co-author of Article 231 now declared, affirming that the Allies 'had enforced on this people at the point of the bayonet the final humiliation of reciting, through the mouths of their representatives, what they believed to be untrue' (JMK 3:27). Yet nobody seems to have seized upon this extraordinary admission, presumably because Keynes's own complicity was not appreciated at that time; and indeed Dulles's role was not fully apparent until his revelations were made public in 1940. Both men were to spend considerable periods of the Second World War in either London or Washington, each now with higher status in conducting inter-governmental business than twenty years previously. But there is no record that they met again in that era. Perhaps they would have been inhibited from doing so by some sense of guilt that was beyond their mutual comprehension.

3

'You Are Very Famous, Maynard'
Keynes and the Manchester Guardian

In the *New York Times*, reporting on the peace negotiations in Paris on 27 May 1919, there had been mention of an obscure member of the British delegation called 'John M. Keynes' – a form of his name that he never used. It was the first time that his name appeared there, to be followed by nearly three hundred subsequent references in the next ten years (compared with about sixty in *The Times* in London). Despite the plethora of controversy provoked by the publication of the *Economic Consequences* in late 1919, and despite the salience of the War Guilt issue, there seems to have been no public recognition of Keynes's full implication in the murky sequence of events in Paris. Nonetheless his career as an academic in Cambridge was now eclipsed by his fame as a polemicist, with prestigious newspapers anxious to seek contributions from him and to print articles that were syndicated throughout the world, not least in the United States. Only in such a context can we understand the origins, the nature and the impact of the notable series of Supplements that the *Manchester Guardian* commissioned under Keynes's editorship, with the general title 'Reconstruction in Europe'.

It was on 12 October 1921 that the editor of the paper, Charles Prestwich Scott, met Keynes face to face. C. P. Scott, at seventy-five, was now a living legend, still sitting in the editor's chair that he had occupied in Manchester for half a century and notorious for having the ear of the Prime Minister, David Lloyd George. Scott's self-appointed role was to act as Lloyd George's liberal conscience when he strayed from the paths of righteousness (though nobody at that time called this speaking truth to power). Scott was also ready to travel to London to meet Keynes, a man half his own age, in order to sell the idea of a series of special supplements. These were to be supervised by Keynes and to be printed not only in Manchester but with translation for French, German, Spanish and Italian editions. This proposal clearly proved attractive, in more senses than one. 'I like the idea and I think I might be able to make a good job of it', Keynes responded after thinking it over for a week. He made it clear that, if he agreed, it would not be a nominal commitment: 'In fact, I am not prepared for my name to appear in a way that implies responsibility unless I can really exercise pretty detailed supervision over the writers' (JMK 17:320).

The proposal held two big attractions and faced two major distractions. The money on offer was obviously attractive, as Keynes immediately made clear to Scott. 'The question of the disposal of the American Rights in the articles is important, for I think they could be disposed of for a very substantial sum, which would have the effect of greatly reducing the burden on you of payment to the authors'. He went into some detail about this before committing himself. 'I suggest that remuneration to myself should be at the rate of £200 per issue, with additional payments for any articles which I should contribute myself' (JMK 17:321). Together with payments for his dozen signed articles, as eventually published,

73

his total remuneration was about £4,000 (say, £180,000 in today's money).

Some comparative perspectives are relevant here: only one of them academic. In the 1920s the annual salary of a Cambridge professor – A. C. Pigou, for example, who now held Alfred Marshall's former chair in economics – was around £1,000 a year; and Keynes was in every way junior to Pigou in the academic hierarchy. But, after the reception of his bestseller on the Paris conference, Keynes was not just an academic economist but an internationally renowned liberal publicist whom Scott very much wanted to recruit. Moreover, even while writing the *Economic Consequences* in the summer of 1919, Keynes's own financial horizons had expanded in a remarkable way. It was when he resigned from the Treasury that he sprang free from staid inhibitions of confidentiality and probity in not only his literary but also his financial enterprises. With unshockable vulgarity, he immediately considered himself free not only to spill the beans but to make a bean or two for himself.

As a Treasury official his salary had been about £1,000 a year; but after his resignation, in the tax year 1919–20, his income was over £5,000 (and was subsequently to fluctuate around such a figure until the mid-1930s, when it went even higher) (JMK 12:2). Hitherto he had learned a lot about the currency markets in the course of his official work on Indian finance, and then in protecting the vulnerable pound sterling under wartime stresses at the Treasury. Within weeks of quitting his government post in Paris, Keynes began speculating on a large scale in the foreign exchange market. Instead of having to look after the interests of Britain's

74

wartime allies – like France and Italy – Keynes now began selling short on their currencies; with impartial composure, he shorted also on the vulnerable German mark; and conversely he bought long on the US dollar. Now he was the gamekeeper turned poacher.

By January 1920, with the *Economic Consequences* eagerly snatched from the shelves of the bookshops, its author hit another high, this time on the foreign exchange markets, realising profits of over £6,000. Of course, it was too good to last. His hunch about the way the markets were moving was to be proved correct in the long run; but in the short run he found himself dead in the water, with actual debts that he could just about clear but also 'moral debts' to family and Bloomsbury friends that he also assumed. By the end of 1922, having gone back unabashed into the market, he had not only paid off all such debts but had personal assets of some £21,000 (say a million pounds today) (Moggridge 1992, 348–51).

Here is the context for the negotiations that he had meanwhile concluded with Scott, putting into perspective the financial terms of his newspaper contract, which were not really a problem. And there was another kind of obvious attraction for Keynes. For in his eyes, the *Manchester Guardian* was not just any old newspaper. The fact that it was published in Manchester rather than in London announced its status, speaking for the commercial and industrial interests of Britain, as it had since the days of the 'Manchester School' with its laissez-faire ethos in the nineteenth century. Until the First World War, Lancashire was still the home of a thriving cotton industry that accounted for over a quarter of Britain's visible exports. A commitment to free trade was shared by both the Liberal Party and the infant Labour Party; Scott had long seen it as his mission to preach the need for a progressive alliance between them, with a common commitment to social reform. Keynes knew, if only from his upbringing in a Liberal household in Harvey Road, that Scott was both editor and proprietor of a newspaper that pre-eminently represented a strain of progressive politics with which Keynes instinctively identified.

Hence the peculiar attractiveness for him of the offer, which Keynes soon accepted despite two intervening distractions. One of these was a prior commitment to go to India to serve on a government commission. This invitation in the summer of 1921 was itself a mark of the political esteem in which Keynes was now held, as well as of his own prior involvement in Indian currency issues. The fact that the invitation came from his old friend and patron, Edwin Montagu, who was now Lloyd George's Secretary of State for India, had no doubt encouraged Keynes to accept; and the personal link likewise made it embarrassing for him to withdraw his consent. But Keynes nonetheless did so in the following January.

For by then there was a further potential distraction, and one of much greater significance in Keynes's life. This was the beginning of his love affair with Lydia Lopokova. She enjoyed, at the time, as much celebrity status as he did: not, of course, as an economist but as a Russian ballerina who had made her name with Diaghilev's *Ballet Russe*. It was in the winter of 1921–2 that the two of them reignited a relationship that was subsequently to result in their improbable but highly successful marriage, once Lydia's legally complicated marital status had been resolved. For Maynard, who had previously confined his romantic attentions to his own sex, this marked a major turning-point in his life. His rather embarrassing withdrawal from his Indian commitment was clearly linked to his suddenly consuming relationship with Lydia.

Moreover, Keynes's decision not to travel to India removed a significant obstacle to proceeding with the Reconstruction Supplements on the timetable desired by C. P. Scott. The old editor's patience was evidently taxed, as shown in his private comment in March 1922 to a trusted friend (J. L. Hammond): 'Keynes is a brilliant and original thinker in his own subjects, but he is also about the most obstinate and self-centred man I ever encountered' (Skidelsky 1992, 102). Perhaps that explains why Scott's two sons in the family business (Ted and John) took over from their father in handling most of the subsequent arrangements. As events turned out, the impact of Lydia upon Maynard's career does not, in the end, constitute a separate chapter from the economist's work for the *Manchester Guardian*; there was a highly significant interaction that had far-reaching consequences.

***

The Reconstruction Supplements began publication on 20 April 1922. In the English edition, they were printed in a format half the size of the ordinary daily editions of the *Manchester Guardian* itself, which was in those days a full broadsheet (approximately 30 inches by 24 inches, or 75 centimetres by 60 centimetres). There were illustrations – a large photograph of Lloyd George in the first issue, for example, with a message conveying his best wishes for the enterprise, printed along with messages from the Prime Ministers of Italy and Czechoslovakia. The articles were printed in three columns to the page, giving a rather crowded look to the modern eye; and Keynes evidently felt some unease. 'I agree that the Supplement looks very fine indeed', he told Ted Scott on receiving the first number. 'My only regret is that it should be of such large dimensions. It is very difficult to handle so large a page combined with so thick a volume' (JMK 17:353).

There were in the end twelve supplements, originally promised to conclude by early October 1922. In fact, the last under Keynes's editorship did not appear until January 1923, completing the enterprise in 782 pages of text. There were also up to fifty pages of advertisements in each issue, often coordinated with the particular themes covered – shipping, textiles, oil, railways, for example – which made good sense in a paper that circulated among businessmen in the north of England. But the international reach of the enterprise was integral. The first number printed – and sold – 30,000 in its English edition, though it seems that the 10,000 printed in German proved over-optimistic; and 4,000 were printed in each of the French, Italian and Spanish translations. 'The financial results are a good deal below expectation (owing to Germany)', Ted Scott told Keynes as the last issue went to press. But he still took an optimistic view of what had been achieved: 'Even if we made a loss of £1000 the *Commercial* will have gained more in circulation than it could possibly have gained by the expenditure of the same amount of money in any other way. Also it has gained enormously, of course, in prestige and future developments will be easier' (JMK 17:447).

The European ambit of the enterprise was essential, as Keynes made clear in his editorial foreword to the first number. 'We offer a forum to Europe', he wrote. 'I dare say that each of our readers, of whatever complexion, will be able to pick out some author as being, in *his* view, very wicked, but I hope that he will also find another whom he will deem perfectly virtuous'. He also admitted that selection of contributors was not random. 'The intellectual forces of Europe will here assemble in order to reinforce those of generous impulse', was how he put it. 'We shall assume that there is nothing wrong in all men talking together; that a common purpose of mutual advantage is not chimerical; and that whatever scares and panics and excommunications may be raised by some, it is quite certain that the patient peoples of Europe are not "plotting" against one another anywhere' (JMK 17:351–2).

In practice this meant that there was an undoubted liberal or left-wing bias among the various contributors. Conversely, the right-wing Prime Minister of France, Raymond Poincaré, with whom Keynes had already clashed over the terms of the Versailles Treaty, could not be recruited to offer support. Since the French edition, for reasons of economy, was printed in Germany and needed official permission to be imported into France, even its circulation in France was under threat at one point. A solution of sorts was found but it is fair to say that the Reconstruction Supplements were somewhat tainted in France by the editor's reputation as author of the *Economic Consequences*. There, the public interventions of Tardieu, Mantoux and, of course, Clemenceau himself all fanned the embers of fires that had been set in Paris in 1919.

The final rollcall of contributors to the Supplements remains impressive – even those from France. The 2nd number (18 May 1922) deliberately included a contribution from the right-wing, Anglophobe diplomat and writer Gabriel Hanotaux – a 'brilliant article', as Keynes hailed it in singling it out for a riposte in his own general introduction (JMK 17:431). The 5th number (27 July 1922) printed contributions from the French left-wingers Léon Blum and Eduard Herriot and also from Joseph Caillaux, who had frequently served as finance minister over the preceding twenty years but whom Poincaré regarded as pro-German, thus reinforcing his own hostility to the project.

This number focussed on the national finances of Europe. It also included articles by Asquith, the former Liberal Prime Minister of the United Kingdom and an early patron of Keynes; by Sidney Webb, the British Fabian socialist; and by Luigi Einaudi, the doyen of Italian economists. In other numbers, there were articles by other eminent European economists, for example Gustav Cassel on Scandinavia, as well as by American financial advisors and publicists with whom Keynes had had previous contacts in Paris, such as R. C. Leffingwell, Walter Lippmann, O. M. W. Sprague and even Thomas Lamont (though not, of course, Bernard Baruch – and not Norman Davis either). Likewise, Carl Melchior, with whom Keynes had established a friendship from the days when Melchior participated in the peace negotiations, gave crucial assistance in recruiting other German contributors as well as by writing himself. Melchior fascinated Keynes – as Lydia Lopokova seems to have sensed even before meeting him herself.

Financial expertise was by no means the only criterion in the selection of contributors. The historian Lewis Namier, now making his name in Britain, was enlisted to write on

Galicia and (later) on the agrarian revolution; another historian, R. H. Tawney, already well-known as a left-wing polemicist, wrote on the coal industry. Nor were the British politicians all Liberals: Lord Robert Cecil was a prominent Conservative supporter of the League of Nations; Ramsay MacDonald was the leader of the Labour Party, Philip Snowden and Arthur Greenwood his colleagues; and intellectual supporters of the Labour Party, including H. J. Laski and G. D. H. Cole, also wrote articles. The contributors whom Keynes recruited, in short, ranged from Dr Hjalmar Schacht, the later architect of financial policy in Hitler's Germany, to the glamorous Queen Marie of Rumania (with a large photograph of her majesty accompanying and fortifying her plea for her adopted country, which she had plainly taken to her bosom).

By the time the first Supplement appeared on 20 April 1922, moreover, regular readers of the *Manchester Guardian* were already thoroughly familiar with the by-line J. M. Keynes. During the previous ten days the paper had printed on its main editorial page a series of special articles by him, sent from the Genoa international conference. This assembly was convened largely at Lloyd George's instigation in hopes of belatedly softening the terms of the Versailles settlement, as imposed by the Allies without any real negotiation after the Armistice; his aim was to bring European leaders together through such conclaves in the watering places of Europe, in a process unkindly dubbed 'casino diplomacy'. At Genoa, for the first time since the war, Germany and Russia, neither of them members of the League of Nations, were invited to participate in an international conference; the other notable non-member, the United States, had declined to attend.

Keynes, although Lloyd George's notorious critic over Versailles, recognised with approval this change of course in British policy. It was naturally applauded also by the *Manchester Guardian* – with the venerable Scott, as usual, acting as keeper of Lloyd George's conscience. It made good sense, then, for the paper to commission Keynes's despatches from Genoa, despite the fact that it also had its own special correspondent, whose anonymous reports conscientiously supplied a less opinionated account of how the conference was proceeding.

The interlocking relationship between Keynes's Genoa despatches and the Reconstruction Supplements is therefore obvious. In fact, his article 'The Stabilisation of the European Exchanges: A Plan for Genoa', appearing in the first Supplement on 20 April, had already been published in the daily edition of the *Manchester Guardian* on 6 April, on the eve of Keynes's departure for Genoa. There were to be twelve of his subsequent despatches from Genoa itself, published between 10 April and 4 May 1922. All of these have been reprinted in the relevant volume of the *Collected Writings*, which is now the accessible modern source, preserving these articles for posterity in a far more satisfactory format than the two densely printed columns on the editorial pages of the *Manchester Guardian* in which they originally appeared, day by day (JMK 17: 370–420).

***

There is, moreover, a further source that allows us a glimpse of the contemporary impact that Keynes's articles made upon one impressionable reader – and also conveys some telling advice to this academic economist about the style in which it was most effective to clothe his thoughts. For Lydia had quickly emerged as a transformative influence in the shaping of Maynard's life in ways that affected the trajectory of his career, not least in the way that he chose to propagate his ideas. She was now living in accommodation that Maynard had acquired in Gordon Square, Bloomsbury, alongside his culturally sympathetic neighbours, notably Clive and Vanessa Bell, Duncan Grant, Lytton Strachey and Leonard and Virginia Woolf.

Lydia's initial relationship with 'Bloomsbury', however, was not easy, especially after her lover had left for Genoa. 'It is very empty Maynard, without your walk of life', she had written to him on the day of his departure, 8 April; and luckily her letters to him for the rest of April 1922 have been preserved (unlike most of his in reply). 'I gobble you my dear Maynard', Lydia wrote on 10 April. 'I am not like you talented in idea put into words, I express myself better in impulses to you' (Hill and Keynes 1989, 31). The intensity of her feelings, and her warm sensuality, are inimitably expressed, in ways that triumph over her eccentric syntax and her idiosyncratic grasp of the English language.

Lydia was well aware that Maynard was not acting exclusively for the *Manchester Guardian*, regarded by her as an unfamiliar highbrow daily newspaper that was irritatingly difficult to obtain in London on the morning of publication. Keynes had in fact arranged for syndication of his articles, well aware of the financial advantages. Hence the misconception, naturally seized upon in the French press and in Conservative newspapers in Britain, that he was in Genoa simply on behalf of a German newspaper. On 15 April he issued his clarification – 'the newspapers for which I am acting as correspondent being the following: the *Manchester Guardian*; the *Daily Express* of London; the *New York World* and Syndicated Press of America; *L'Ère Nouvelle*; *Corriere della Sera* of Milan; *Berliner Tageblatt*; *Prager Presse*; *Neue Freie Presse* of Vienna; *Algemeen Handelsblad* of Amsterdam; *Dagens Nyheter* of Stockholm' (JMK 17:380).

'So very famous', Lydia had commented on 12 April, with admiration (though also with some disappointment that her own picture had only appeared in the popular newspaper the *Daily Express*) (Hill and Keynes 1989, 32). It was a couple of days before she caught up with the published version of Maynard's first despatch from Genoa, which she specially commended. The style Maynard now adopted was hardly that of an academic economist. 'Not much flourish of trumpets this time', was how he began and he was positively theatrical in setting the scene. 'The British prime minister steps on the stage, no longer clothed in the imperial purple with the emblems of victory and omnipotence, but in the drab garment of an itinerant friar, weary, sorrowful for the world, a preacher; or as another Charles V, on his way to the monastery of Yuste, taking Genoa en route' (JMK 17:370).

The essential conflict, Keynes maintained, was not a struggle between Russian Bolshevism and 'the bourgeois states of the nineteenth-century type'. It was instead, in his view, 'between that view of the world, termed liberalism or radicalism, for which the primary object of government and of foreign policy is peace, freedom of trade and intercourse, and economic wealth, and that other view, militarist or, rather, diplomatic, which thinks in terms of power, prestige, national or personal glory, the imposition of a culture, and hereditary or racial prejudice'. Any contest between a bourgeois and a socialist form of state was a secondary struggle to be measured by their relative efficiency in generating the economic wealth of the community. 'Soldiers and diplomatists – they are the permanent, the immortal foe' (JMK 17:373). The confident pejorative stereotyping sounded very much like that identifying the 'eternal secretary of state' whom he had satirised in his first book on Indian currency.

The chief significance of the Genoa conference, as it seemed to Keynes on his arrival, lay in the fact that both Germany and Russia had duly accepted their invitations to attend. In particular, the Russian representative, Georgy Chicherin, was identified as a key figure. Distantly related to Pushkin, Chicherin came from a noble family; he was himself homosexual and now well established as Soviet foreign minister (1918–30). He was a worldly, cultured figure whom Keynes found sympathetic and the fact that Chicherin had brought with him copies of not only the *Economic Consequences* but also its sequel, *A Revision of the Treaty*, obviously ingratiated him with the author. Keynes used the *Manchester Guardian* to commend Chicherin, along with Lloyd George, as the two statesmen quick-witted enough to rescue the conference from the usual stalemate.

On many of the international financial issues, Keynes was thus playing a double game, now himself working upon the reconciliation of inside and outside opinion. He was, as an acknowledged expert, confidentially urging upon the British delegation his own plans for currency reform, while simultaneously, as a journalist, writing despatches in support. Lydia's comment, that 'you always go in advance of all the others' may betray some naivety in her admiring comments; but she was right to seize on the prominence of his role. 'You are very famous, Maynard' (Hill and Keynes 1989, 34).

This famous economist went on to evoke from the Russian ballerina an even warmer response when he tackled the subject of the old tsarist debts, left over from the war and repudiated by the Bolshevik regime. For Poincaré's France, with its million aggrieved bondholders, this was hardly less of an issue than Germany's liability for the payment of reparations under the Versailles Treaty. From his own perspective, Keynes made the same comparison, but suggested that 'Russian debt is a miserable repetition of reparations and inter-Allied debt'. He pointed to the hollowness of the Anglo-French demand: not a request for the actual payment of the supposed milliards of money at stake, but merely a demand for 'recognition' of the debt by Russia – 'just as we successfully pressed Germany to repeat words which certainly did not express sincere intention'. Here, evidently, was the fatal flaw of 'insincerity' that he had identified in the *Economic Consequences* – the common taint of humbug in the treatment of Germany and Russia alike. 'We act as high priests, not debt collectors', Keynes mockingly commented. 'The heretics must repeat our creed' (JMK 17:388). Yet did he ever pause to consider whether, in their work on the 'well and carefully drafted' Article 231, he and Dulles had likewise been demanding that the Germans 'repeat our creed' by formally signing the War Guilt Clause? (see JMK 2:95).

This despatch, Keynes's fifth as correspondent and filed on Monday 17 April 1922, was printed in the next day's

Manchester Guardian, headlined 'Rubbish about Milliards'. It was duly applauded by Lydia in London, appreciative of the sympathy shown for her compatriots; but by then, as she could now read in the main news column of the same day's paper, events had moved on in a dramatic way. For what threw everything into disarray in Genoa was that the Germans and Russians had meanwhile slipped away for the Easter weekend for a bilateral meeting at nearby Rapallo, where they had signed a treaty of mutual recognition, cancelling outstanding financial claims between them. This move, which certainly gave Chicherin the initiative, effectively upstaged the Genoa conference itself.

It took some adroit footwork by Lloyd George to salvage the work of the international gathering that he had himself summoned. As in Paris in the early summer of 1919, this great pragmatist saw his role as that of making the best of bad situation; and, now as then, the real question was how far the French could be brought to an accommodation over all outstanding debts. Any idea of wiping the slate clean at this point would not be condoned by a French government, least of all by one under Poincaré, who sat out most of the conference in Paris, fearful of any personal contagion from Lloyd George.

In his despatches, Keynes blamed the Germans rather than the Russians for any breach of faith in concluding their Rapallo Treaty. In London, as ever, he found at least one appreciative reader of his proposal on a Russian settlement. 'I do want it to be adopted. It is clever', Lydia assured him. 'When I read what you write somehow I feel bigger than I am' (Hill and Keynes 1989, 35). Keynes also put some of the blame on the British Prime Minister, for having talked mainly to the other wartime Allies – 'he should have remembered that M. Chicherin is one of the most brilliant diplomatists in Europe and by no means in the position of a vanquished suppliant' (JMK 17:396). The *Manchester Guardian*, though always inclined to give Lloyd George the benefit of the doubt, backed up its correspondent in this reading of the situation, with supportive leading articles on both 18 and 19 April.

This helpful orchestration reached its climax on Thursday 20 April 1922. The *Manchester Guardian* now printed a further sympathetic editorial alongside Keynes's seventh despatch on page 6 of the paper; not only that, but on page 4 there was half a page advertising the first number of the Reconstruction Supplements, published that day. Best of all, on page 8 of the paper a photograph displayed the debonair figure of its new man in Genoa, respectably clad in his homburg hat, with his waistcoat and his watch-chain, and carrying his walking stick. 'Another surprise – you in M.G. quite a big photo', wrote Lydia. 'Very famous!' (Hill and Keynes 1989, 36; the despatch is misdated 21 April in JMK 17:394; the photograph appears as frontispiece to that volume).

***

The launch of the *Manchester Guardian* Reconstruction Supplements could hardly have had more loyal support. We do not have Maynard's letters to Lydia at this point but we can surely infer from her responses that he must have evinced some modesty (real or affected) about his efforts, thus earning her reprimand: 'Do not speak against your articles in journalism – just think how many peoples read, understand and remember it; and when you go to bed have the feeling of the work you have done with mind and inspiration' (Hill and Keynes 1989, 36). Lydia was clearly pleased that Maynard was devoting so much attention to Russia in his later despatches, those published on 26 April, 1 May and 4 May especially. She approved too of their tone of sceptical sympathy towards the Bolshevik experiment.

Chicherin indeed emerged from Keynes's despatches as the most impressive figure at the conference, entitled to 'retire home with dignity and an enhanced prestige' as a statesman who was both 'astute and skilful' (JMK 17:419). But any chauvinism on Lydia's part was, in the end, less significant than her influence in encouraging Maynard to communicate his ideas in an idiom that would reach a wide readership. When the first Reconstruction Supplement appeared, Keynes was still in Genoa and was to contribute five further despatches over the next two weeks. By then he had fulfilled his contract as correspondent to the newspaper, even if the conference was still limping on. His own proposals for currency reform, seeking to internationalise policies of stabilisation in a reformed version of the gold standard, had gone nowhere in the end. In rather the same mood that he had quit Paris before the peace conference was finished in 1919, he returned to England at the beginning of May 1922.

Keynes now devoted his energies that summer into making his ideas as persuasive as possible to the thousands of readers across Europe who had by this time subscribed to the *Manchester Guardian* Supplements on the Reconstruction of Europe. The protean problem of international debt on which debate focussed was generated by the war, and was now faced alike by the successor regimes in Germany and Russia (whose public reconciliation at Rapallo thus had its own logic).

Keynes had already spoken, with considerable influence, on the German problem: as he saw it, the impact of a demand for reparations that would never be paid by Germany, and hence never received by France. In his introduction to the Reconstruction Supplements, he contested Hanotaux's notion that the Frenchman's local mayor, still condemned to living in the cellar of his war-damaged house, had a justified reproach against the unfeeling author of the *Economic Consequences* for not helping him to rebuild the house. Hence Keynes's riposte: 'I protest in the name of good sense and our own interests, and tell the mayor very confidently that his house will be rebuilt much sooner by my economics than by the sentimental miscalculations of M. Poincaré' (JMK 17:432). In the 8th number of the Reconstruction Supplements Keynes returned to his theme, dismissing 'the fallacy, which deceives many Frenchmen, that the extremity of France's need enlarges Germany's capacity' (JMK 18:33). In short, his analysis rested on the perception that this was not in fact a zero-sum game, however prevalent the misconceptions to the contrary.

The economic consequences for Russia became central to Keynes's agenda in 1922, as he made clear to readers of the *Manchester Guardian*. 'If we practise on Russia what we have already practised on Germany, and compel her under force of economic pressure to recite a promise which she cannot keep and which we know she does not mean to keep, we shall have disgraced ourselves' (JMK 17:391). He was confident that a settlement of the old Russian debts to the bondholders was possible. His premise here (again a message unwelcome to French ears) was that private investors had no right to any public guarantees: 'Those who lent money to the tsar's government took a big risk' (JMK 17:391). In short, having lost their bet against history, such investors needed to take a haircut in order to allow the world to move on. Problems of debt as between different parts of Europe needed rational solutions at an inter-governmental level, writing down debts that would never be collected in order to liberate and stimulate the forces of economic recovery. Little wonder that what Keynes wrote at this time has been rediscovered with a renewed sense of relevance in the era of the euro.

Keynes's verdict on the Genoa conference was given in the 3rd number of the Reconstruction Supplements, published in June 1922. It was double-edged, specifically about the role of Lloyd George. As we have seen, Keynes had already published, in his *Revision of the Treaty*, a possible extenuation of Lloyd George's characteristic pragmatism, as an expedient strategy for achieving his objectives by stealth and at the expense of literal truth. 'The political government of the world is dragged along by two horses, equally ill-mated in tandem or in yoke', Keynes now reiterated this point. 'The creation of atmosphere, the development of public sentiment, the precise emotional suggestion of the cant phrases of the hour, the gradual shifting of what it is correct for the conventional person to think and say – these things are very important; but chiefly *as a means* to make possible the other task of government – a right policy of action' (JMK 17:420–1, italics in original). He thus allowed Lloyd George some credit, if only for achieving the first of these objectives in his policy at Genoa. 'But if we regard it not as propaganda but as an attempt to draw up a well-considered plan for the economic reconstruction of Europe, then the unfavourable judgment of the world must be accepted' (JMK 17:421–2).

***

The point about Keynes's journalism is not just that he found that he was good at it, nor that it earned him sums of money that elevated him far above the income of a professor of economics, nor that he was indeed famous as a result. Its continuing relevance is also that we can find in his journalism the origins of many of his animating ideas. Moreover, when he developed such ideas later, in less ephemeral publications for a more professional readership, he did so in a manner that henceforth carried the imprint of his style as a journalist – arresting in expression, striving for simplicity in exposition, with few arcane allusions that would only appeal to a highly educated readership, but instead with a spontaneous resort to the vernacular in clinching his arguments.

The evidence can be seen in the fourth volume of the *Collected Writings*, reprinting Keynes's book *A Tract on Monetary Reform* (1923), which deals with complex issues in economic policy and international finance. The familiar quotation for which Keynes became popularly known to the general public – '*In the long run* we are all dead' – is a sentence that first appeared in Chapter 3. Yet the very next paragraph duly reverts to an altogether different vocabulary: 'In actual experience, a change of n is liable to have a reaction both on k and k' and on r' (JMK 4:65). Keynes evidently had more than one way of mounting such arguments.

The *Tract* certainly earned the respect of some of the most rigorous academic economists of the day. 'The book will differ from my other recent volumes', Keynes had explained to his publisher, 'in that it will be suitable for use as a textbook in universities, and as it contains a considerable amount of new matter adapted either for advanced or relatively elementary work I think it might have a considerable vogue as time goes on for this purpose' (JMK 19:77). Yet this purported economics textbook had its origin as journalism. Moreover, the annotated edition of the *Tract* that we use today, in the *Collected Writings*, helpfully allows us to identify the precise extent to which Keynes modified his original articles.

That he modified them so little is itself remarkable. True, Keynes put in a prefatory note acknowledging his use of 'the material, much revised and rewritten, of some articles which were published during 1922 in the Reconstruction Supplements of the *Manchester Guardian Commercial*' (JMK 4:xii). But this formula made light of his borrowings from the Supplements; the revision and rewriting was trivial – a word changed here or there – throughout a substantial part of the book. The first chapter, 'The consequences to society of changes in the value of money' (JMK 4:1–36), follows the text of a long article in the 5th number of the Supplements, 27 July 1922. The second chapter, 'Public finance and changes in the value of money' (JMK 4:37–42), follows, paragraph by paragraph, an earlier article in this 5th number, thus inverting their original sequence but otherwise printing substantially the same text, except for a variant ending (with the original printed as an appendix in the modern edition) (JMK 4:161–3).

And so it goes on. The third chapter, 'The theory of money and the exchanges', after a new beginning, prints a version of another of the articles that Keynes had published in the Supplement's first number (JMK 4: 70–80). After some divergence, this chapter reverts to a substantial borrowing from a further article in the first Supplement (JMK 4:94–115). While Chapters 4 and 5 of the *Tract* are indeed new, the first three chapters, running to about eighty pages – no less than half the book – represent only a very light reworking of what had first appeared under the auspices of the *Manchester Guardian*.

There is nothing disreputable in this. After all, the notion of self-plagiarism is itself a contradiction in terms; and in the era of the computer few writers will hesitate to 'copy-and-paste' as convenient – except that Keynes had to do this literally with scissors and glue to hand. Moreover, as author of the *Tract* he offered some acknowledgement of his debt; and there was no conflict of interest with the original publisher. The *Manchester Guardian* felt sufficiently rewarded for its own role in publishing the twelve Reconstruction Supplements under Keynes's editorship, stating in the final number on 4 January 1923: 'The reception accorded to what has been described as "the most ambitious journalistic venture of modern times" has been very gratifying'. Keynes's contract with the *Manchester Guardian*, moreover, had always protected his own rights to republication of his own articles. 'You indicated to me in conversation', he had purposefully reminded C. P. Scott back in October 1921, 'that the idea of possible republication did not much interest you, as it will be a trifling affair compared with the main project and a complication not worth bothering about' (JMK 17:322). For himself, as he already sensed, the balance of comparative advantage tipped the other way.

Much as he had valued the opportunity to assume the editorship of this great enterprise, then, his perspective was not just that of a journalist, nor even that of an economist who was slumming. As an economist, he knew that his impact would finally be measured and enhanced by what appeared in print between hard covers. Crucially, the process of editing the Supplements for the *Manchester Guardian*, and of simultaneously representing the newspaper at the Genoa conference, enhanced his consciousness of the gifts of expression that these tasks stimulated in him. As Lydia had assured Maynard, his adventure in journalism was not to be despised. What he wrote for the *Manchester Guardian* in 1922 addressed current issues of the moment; it did so in a style that had an immediacy that made a vivid impression. But in doing so, it also stimulated a kind of analysis that has an enduring relevance for us a hundred years later, when problems of international debt still sunder Europe and the wider world in various intractable forms.

[Original files of the *Manchester Guardian* and the *Manchester Guardian Commercial Supplements* were consulted in the Cambridge University Library – dates as given in the text. There are useful sections on the Supplements in Harrod (1951, 315–16); Skidelsky (1992, 102–6); and Moggridge (1992, 376–9).]

4

The Truth About Lloyd George

Four Perspectives

When Keynes published *A Revision of the Treaty* in 1922, as we have seen, it might as well have been called *A Revision of My View of Lloyd George*. Partly this was a retrospective qualification to the harsh judgements offered in the *Economic Consequences*, implying that Keynes had meanwhile changed his mind. But it was also an adjustment to a changed situation, now that the Prime Minister was no longer pandering to the right-wing populism of the Coupon Election but instead embarking on his 'casino diplomacy', just like a good revisionist liberal, in the changing state of public opinion when the truth could now be acknowledged. Lloyd George was thus engaged in 'protecting Europe from as many of the evil consequences of his own Treaty, as it lay in his power to prevent, with a craft few could have bettered, preserving the peace, though not the prosperity, of Europe, seldom expressing the truth, yet often acting under its influence' (JMK 3:2).

In the course of their long relationship, extending through a quarter of a century from their first meeting in 1914, there were many plausible contemporary perspectives on Lloyd George; and Keynes expressed at least four of them, which I propose to review in sequence rather than seeking to reconcile them. Moreover, just as Keynes had distinguished between inside opinion and outside opinion, it is important to discriminate between what he himself observed and expressed in private and what he chose to say in public at any one time. Thus the forum in which he shared his thoughts with close friends in Bloomsbury provided a context where Maynard was licensed to shock and to tease; but it was a different matter if Keynes, as a public figure himself from 1919, chose to publish his candid comments on Lloyd George – especially if he hoped to work with him, whether in revising the reparations proposals of the Treaty or in devising policies for tackling unemployment.

It is surely no coincidence that, when Keynes cast off his self-consciously academic mien and wrote in his more accessible style, he often wrote about Lloyd George. This was obviously true in his journalism, of course, if only because Lloyd George was always in the news at the time, whether as the Man Who Won the War, as peace-maker, as British Prime Minister or (from 1926 to 1931) as leader of the Liberal Party. But Keynes's fascination with Lloyd George was not contingent on the title or office that Lloyd George held at any one particular time. Instead, it was a reflection of the profound but ambivalent impact made upon Keynes when he observed at close quarters a unique sort of mastery of the art of politics – one that transcended mere intellectual analysis or conventional moral judgement. Above Lloyd George's bed in Downing Street hung a text from the Book of Job: 'There is a path which no fowl knoweth and which the eye of the vulture hath not seen' (Jones 1951, title page). Keynes, who could hardly have known this, often groped for a way of conveying such a sense of Lloyd George's intuitive tactical mastery, notably in the 'post-truth' register of *A Revision of the Treaty*:

'He would claim, therefore, that by devious paths, a faithful servant of the possible, he was serving man' (JMK 3:2).

Even though the *Economic Consequences* had indeed been scornful of Lloyd George in many passages, especially on his electioneering in December 1918, it simultaneously displayed more than a sneaking admiration for his political skills. In the famous third chapter, the portrait of Clemenceau, acknowledged as 'by far the most eminent member of the Council of Four', is an artistic triumph in its depiction of a man dedicated to salvaging French interests in a perpetual zero-sum game against Germany. 'He felt about France what Pericles felt of Athens – unique value in her, nothing else mattering; but his theory of politics was Bismarck's' (JMK 2:18, 20). Everything else followed from this. And Keynes actually had far more sympathy for the sufferings of France than is normally credited; so there is keen critical observation but no malice in his portraiture.

President Wilson, as we have seen, was much more the target of the author's disdain, for purporting to uphold a liberal agenda that he was in fact incapable of fulfilling. And it was Wilson's vanity that prevented him from acknowledging the concessions that might justifiably be made to expediency. 'The President, for me, was a fallen hero', Keynes told Norman Davis. 'I describe the others as very clever and very wicked; the President as sincere, well-intentioned and determined to do what was right, but perplexed, muddleheaded and a self-deceiver' (JMK 17:42). It is this perspective that made the book's depiction of Wilson so deadly and so offensive to his loyal adherents (like Davis), because here the personal is political.

Not so with Lloyd George whose populist politics at the time, pandering to a wave of nationalist sentiment for electoral reasons, are indeed seen as reprehensible – but in ways that were arguably necessary in appeasing outside opinion at that moment. Hence the double-edged quality of some of the most quotable comments Keynes published on Lloyd George, even in 1919:

> To see the British Prime Minister watching the company, with six or seven senses not available to ordinary men, judging character, motive, and subconscious impulse, perceiving what each was thinking and even what each was going to say next, and compounding with telepathic instinct the argument or the appeal best suited to the vanity, weakness, or self-interest of his immediate auditor, was to realise that the poor President would be playing blind man's buff in that party. (JMK 2:26)

Reading this today, we can indeed still marvel at such political skills – but also at the literary relish with which these are conveyed by the author. Indeed Keynes had drafted a further section, which disclosed his image of 'this syren, this goat-footed bard, this half-human visitor to our age from the hag-ridden magic and enchanted woods of Celtic antiquity'. He indulged in comments on 'that flavour of final purposelessness, inner irresponsibility, existence outside or away from our Saxon good and evil, mixed with cunning, remorselessness, love of power' in this depiction (JMK 10:23). These luxuriant passages by Maynard had been read, along with the rest of the text, by his mother, Florence Keynes, who advised that 'all the nasty hits at Lloyd George' should be eliminated: 'You owe some loyalty to your Chief, even if you don't agree with him' (Skidelsky 1983, 383). Whether swayed by her advice, or that of the former Liberal Prime Minister Asquith to the same effect, Maynard paid homage to discretion and put his draft on Lloyd George into a drawer, where it rested safe from outside eyes during the next twelve years. The *Economic Consequences* did not need this excess of spice (or spite) to achieve its spectacular impact on publication.

In August 1921 Keynes received a letter from Lytton Strachey, a long-standing close friend both in Cambridge and Bloomsbury, and now himself celebrated as the author of *Eminent Victorians*. This had been published a year before the *Economic Consequences* and was in some ways an exemplar for the iconoclastic style adopted in Keynes's portrayal of the Big Three in Paris. So Strachey was well qualified to offer his ironic comment: 'I foresee that 1000 years hence the manuals of English literature will point out that it is important to distinguish between the two entirely distinct authors of the same name, one of whom wrote the Economic Consequences of the Peace, and the other a Treatise on Probability' (Moggridge 1992, 143). Any surprise that Strachey affected – and he was a master of affectation, of course – was more in revulsion at the severe academic style of *Probability* than in doubt about Maynard's ability to conjure his own effects in the biographical vignettes of the *Economic Consequences*.

***

Before Keynes ever went to the Paris conference, he had already been privileged with an earlier perspective on Lloyd George. They shared a history that always coloured their shifting views of each other over time: what they chose to remember and what to forget in their very different careers. What Lloyd George never forgot was that he was an outsider – the cottage-bred boy from a village in Celtic north Wales, who would sometimes choose to call himself a country attorney, and had nonetheless thrust his way to the top in British politics. As he claimed in his *War Memoirs*, 'there had never before been a "ranker" raised to the Premiership – certainly not one except Disraeli who had not passed through the Staff College of the old Universities' (Lloyd George, *WM* 1:621). He relished the fact that he had been brought up as a Baptist in chapel-going, Welsh-speaking north Wales in an era when Nonconformity sustained the Liberal Party and the Church of England was 'the Tory party at prayer'.

Keynes, by contrast, was surely an insider. True, he had gone with his parents to the Emmanuel Congregationalist church in Cambridge as a boy, but then ceased to attend; and, in due course, his two siblings likewise; and subsequently, silently, his parents too (Keynes 1981, 20). Maynard's family roots in the Dissenting tradition were overlaid by his own privileged education at Eton and King's College, Cambridge; his first steps as an economist eased by the patronage of a family friend, Alfred Marshall, the iconic leader of the profession; his wartime career in the Treasury facilitated by useful contacts – one of which, in particular, he chose to acknowledge.

'I am a little sad at the death of Edwin Montagu', Maynard wrote to Lydia in 1924. 'I owed – rather surprisingly – nearly all my steps up in life to him'. He had worked closely with Montagu in Paris, as we have seen, entrusted with doing Lloyd George's dirty work especially in crucial dealings with the Americans. They drew upon a long friendship;

indeed Maynard admitted to Lydia that he had initially been virtually a protégé of the well-connected Montagu. 'It was he who introduced me to the great ones (I first met Lloyd George in a famous dinner party of 4 at his house)' (Hill and Keynes 1989, 256).

Four years older than Keynes, Montagu had been President of the Union Society at Cambridge, picking out Keynes as a freshman to speak in its debates, on the Liberal side of course. Montagu's election as a Cambridgeshire MP in 1906 had been aided by Keynes's speeches on the stump, Nonconformist village by Nonconformist village. Keynes's appointment to the Royal Commission on Indian Finance and Currency in 1913 had come through Montagu, by then a junior minister at the India Office. It was not coincidental that in Keynes's book *Indian Currency and Finance*, which had been rushed into print before the Commission began its sittings, its otherwise dispassionate tone is abandoned at one point. There are a couple of pages of scathing invective about an unfounded recent scandal over the City firm that handled government transactions in silver. 'Unfortunately the head of this firm was closely related by blood to the parliamentary under-secretary of state'. This was Montagu, of course, unnamed but indeed a brother of the senior partner of the bullion brokers Samuel Montagu & Co, and thus a target in this noisy political campaign. 'It was discovered that a number of the most prominent members of the London money market were Jews', Keynes wrote in mock-horror (JMK 1:101–2). His defence of Montagu can be seen as a bold and honourable exposure of anti-Semitism, of which the Marconi scandal, impugning the conduct of Jewish members of the Liberal government as well as Lloyd George's probity as Chancellor of the Exchequer, was another contemporary example. Asquith, as Prime Minister, defended them all, notably his indispensable Chancellor.

It would be difficult to argue that Keynes's own career suffered in the process, with his appointment to a Royal Commission at under thirty giving him access to higher levels of the civil service than when he had briefly been a mere clerk in the India Office. He was indeed a net beneficiary from Montagu's continuing patronage. On the outbreak of war in 1914, what with Keynes's Whitehall contacts through his Royal Commission work and Montagu's recent appointment as Financial Secretary at the Treasury, such connections were again helpful.

It was thus Keynes's advice that was sought in August 1914, unofficially through an obliging friend in the Treasury (Basil Blackett), on how to cope with the threat of a sterling crisis. The key issue was whether to suspend specie payment, meaning the Bank of England's obligation to pay out gold. Keynes wrote a memorandum, advising against suspension, which was shown to the Chancellor. Blackett's diary tells us that Lloyd George 'asked who Keynes was & on being told that he was a friend of mine expert in currency said that it was monstrous that Treasury officials should call in outsiders on their own responsibility. But he read the memorandum' (Roberts 2013, 126).

There is little doubt of the effect in August 1914; the Bank Act was not suspended and the Treasury rode out the crisis. Maynard seems to have been justified in boasting to his father that 'my memorandum converted Lloyd George' (JMK

16:16). Further letters home chart his rapid rise once Montagu was able to engineer a formal appointment for Keynes at the Treasury, starting on 18 January 1915. 'After a slack beginning', he reported four days later, 'I am now very busy, having become Secretary of a Secret Committee of the Cabinet, presided over by the Prime Minister' (JMK 16:57). This was his first encounter with Asquith, whom Keynes duly met socially through Montagu, still at that point Lloyd George's deputy at the Treasury as Financial Secretary. 'I *am* to go to Paris, and we start Sunday or Monday', Maynard told his father at the end of January 1915. 'It's a most select party: Lloyd George, Montagu, the Governor of the Bank of England, and me, together with a secretary' (JMK 16:66, italics in original).

Hence the 'famous dinner party for 4', hosted by Montagu the night before they left, which was Keynes's introduction to Lloyd George in person. Within a fortnight Keynes thus enjoyed face-to-face contact with the two leaders whose rivalry was to contribute to the demise of the Liberal Party over the next fifteen years; and it was only right for him to acknowledge to Lydia how these useful connections had been made. Like Montagu, Keynes was an Asquithian, though both of them were to find themselves working with Lloyd George in the wartime coalition government formed by Asquith in May 1915.

At the Treasury, it was the Asquithian Reginald McKenna who now took over as Chancellor of the Exchequer, while Lloyd George went to the new Ministry of Munitions, charged with mobilising the industrial resources of the country for all-out warfare. This set the terms of a power struggle between the economic demands of Lloyd George's 'great-gun' strategy and the Treasury's insistence that this was unaffordable in terms of either finance or manpower. And it was Keynes who was put up to argue the Treasury's position that 'the limitation of our resources are in sight; and that, in the case of any expenditure, we must consider not only as heretofore, whether it would be useful, but also whether we can afford it' (Lloyd George, *WM* 1:409). It was a passage that Lloyd George subsequently quoted gleefully in his *War Memoirs* as exemplifying a style of argument that failed to comprehend the realities of a wartime economy capable of more elastic expansion under wartime demand. 'The Treasury View', as it was later to be dubbed by Keynes in the 1920s, took this negative view about the capacity available; and the young Keynes indeed acted as its spokesman.

And not unwillingly at the time. We should not assume that Keynes, who had originally aimed at securing a Treasury post when he sat the civil service examinations in 1906, might not have settled for a distinguished administrative career there. His mentor Alfred Marshall, though hoping that this promising academic economist would not (rather like his father) 'abandon science for administration', nonetheless found such an alternative career path highly plausible. He told Keynes in June 1917 that:

> [Y]ou have a better chance than any economist has
> ever had in this country of rendering high services
> to the State on critical occasions; for you will know
> more of economics than any professional statesman
> has done; and you will know more of Whitehall
> difficulties – whether founded in the nature of things
> or in bureaucracy – than any professional economist
> has ever done. (JMK 16:223)

Keynes's own view of the Treasury is revealingly expressed in a lecture that he gave to the Society of Civil Servants in 1921. To this sympathetic audience, the cream of Whitehall, Keynes lauded 'Treasury control' over expenditure, with all the ingrained cultural reflexes of a civil servant *manqué*. He continued to express regret that Treasury control had broken down in wartime – 'There were, of course, innumerable enthusiasts who believed that they could win the war if only they could spend unlimited sums of money' (JMK 16:301). Here was a viewpoint framed in cultural rather than economic terms. For Keynes indulgently commended the Treasury's calculated deployment of prestige, aided by ritual. 'Things could only be done in a certain way, and that made a great many things impossible, which was the object aimed at', Keynes approvingly suggested. It was thus 'an institution which came to possess attributes of institutions like a college or a City company, or the Church of England' (JMK 16:299). This is surely the Fellow of King's College speaking, as an insider to other insiders. The idea that Lloyd George would have been captivated by such an ethos was absurd, as Keynes recognised; and when he himself came to join hands with Lloyd George in the 1920s in denouncing 'the Treasury View', he did so as an apostate.

***

A third perspective on Lloyd George was one that Keynes was more than happy to reveal to the Memoir Club. Established with thirteen founder members in 1920, it was an institution which saw Keynes sitting comfortably alongside other authors of the literary standing of Virginia Woolf and

E. M. Forster, as well as Lytton Strachey. Here was the core membership of 'Bloomsbury': an informal group of friends who lived in houses around the formal squares of this early example of inner London gentrification. And when they chose to define themselves institutionally – a clique masquerading here as a seminar – it was evidently by making the personal memoir their emblematic literary form.

During the years that Virginia Stephen (as she then was) spent growing up in respectable Kensington, she had been given an education by her famous father Leslie that was in many respects scandalously inadequate in developing her own obvious talents. No place at a Cambridge college for her, unlike her brothers, despite the fact that Leslie Stephen had made his early career as a reforming don at Trinity Hall, Cambridge – an episode on which he had anonymously published a series of informal and irreverent essays at the time in his *Cambridge Sketches* (1865). Subsequently, his own aptitude for the spare rigour of the biographical memoir as a form could be seen in the successive volumes that he produced as the founder-editor of the vast *Dictionary of National Biography*. His ghost was surely present at many meetings of the Memoir Club, however much he would have been scandalised by some of its revelations.

Many of Virginia's own early writings were within this diverse and elastic genre. Her evocation of the environment in which she had been brought up, '22 Hyde Park Gate', was read to an early meeting of the Memoir Club in December 1920. Its satirical rendering of the Stephen family household achieves its effects through the sly touches of an impressionistic style that any reader of her subsequent novel

To the Lighthouse (1927) will immediately recognise. There is social comment here but also a forgiving allowance for personal idiosyncrasy, more often conveyed by implication than in direct comment.

The portrait of George Duckworth is central: her much older half-brother who had assumed a quasi-paternal role in the family after Leslie Stephen had become a testy and withdrawn widower. George is mocked for his social pretensions – his self-conscious status as Austen Chamberlain's private secretary an obvious target – but also emerges as a pathetic figure to whom some exasperated sympathy might have been extended. Or at least the members of the Memoir Club could well have been lulled into such indulgent thoughts until Virginia came to read out her shock ending, alleging that 'George Duckworth was not only father and mother, brother and sister to those poor Stephen girls; he was their lover also' (Woolf 2002, 42).

While she read it, a former civil servant who had recently resigned from the Treasury was there listening, obviously impressed. And Keynes again brought it up a few months later, in the course of a long conversation with the author, as she recorded in her diary: 'The best thing you ever did, he said, was your Memoir on George. You should pretend to write about real people & make it all up' – a comment that she took amiss but which surely offers some insight on his own perceptions about an art form in which both of them excelled in different ways (VWD 2:121).

It was, then, a meeting of the Memoir Club to which Maynard gave his own paper 'Dr Melchior: A Defeated Enemy' in February 1921. 'I was a little bored by the politics, &

a good deal impressed by the method of character drawing', wrote Virginia, and even she admitted that the passage on 'L.G. at the table, overwhelmed by his own eloquence' worked well. 'All this was very brilliantly told' (VWD 2:89). True, this great critic of the Prime Minister had, within the elastic form of this digressive memoir, sought not only to tell but also to show his audience exactly how effective Lloyd George could be in action. 'He can be amazing when one agrees with him' (JMK 10:419).

Keynes's memoir 'Dr Melchior: A Defeated Enemy' is some forty pages long – the Woolfs went home before the end and had to read the rest later – and it is also rather uneven in quality. Much of the early part is frankly laborious in setting the scene for Keynes's first meeting with Carl Melchior, a banker who was part of a German delegation negotiating on the application of the Armistice terms in early 1919. Keynes went on behalf of the British Treasury to this meeting at the border town of Trier – his first post-war visit to Germany – because he had been tipped off that the French, led by the great Marshal Foch, had set up a clandestine meeting. Their plan was to introduce control of Germany's gold reserves as a prior condition for the Allies' release of promised food supplies. Keynes's source in Paris had been his then close ally Norman Davis. The two of them had apparently decided that 'it would be extremely amusing and perhaps useful if we stepped onboard the Marshal's train on his journey', giving them ample opportunity to discover their mutual enthusiasm for playing bridge (and evidently for playing the markets too) (JMK 10:391).

The memoir's narrative unfolds slowly. Even the account of that first glimpse of Melchior, when Keynes records 'an extraordinary impression that he was truthful', seems slightly laboured (JMK 10:403). It is with his account of further encounters involving Melchior that the story really comes alive, and not only because (perhaps as a crowd-pleasing sop for the Memoir Club) Keynes added: 'In a sort of way I was in love with him' (JMK 10:415). Woolf commented in her diary that 'I think he meant it seriously, though we laughed' (VWD 2:90).

The memoir's story was intractably complicated. After much prevarication on both sides, stretching over several weeks, a further negotiation had been convened, in Spa on the Belgian frontier, during which Keynes and Melchior met clandestinely. The crux was that each had to trust the sincerity of the other in striking a deal that could not be openly acknowledged on either side. The Germans needed to believe that the Allies would release food supplies provided that they complied with the Armistice terms to hand over their ships; so Melchior was faced with taking Keynes's word for it, while Keynes was faced with persuading Lloyd George that German compliance would indeed follow if the food stocks could be released. There was meanwhile the political theatre of a staged breakdown in the Spa negotiations. The focus then shifted to getting agreement on a common Allied position from the Supreme War Council. So Keynes returned to Paris, working now with the agreeably compliant British Admiral Hope, to explain the tentative understanding that had been reached and secure the *quid pro quo*.

'Our reports won over the Prime Minister', Keynes's memoir tells us (JMK 10:416). Thus he had put into Lloyd George's hand a card that gave him confidence in browbeating the French – the Americans were already onside. 'At last our business was reached', Keynes recounts, almost breathlessly in describing his own presence at this plenary session, with Lloyd George in one of the front-row seats: 'Admiral Hope and I crouched behind the Prime Minister's chair' (JMK 10:417–18). Here is the context for his description of Lloyd George's 'extraordinary powers', once he stirred himself to exercise these at the right moment. 'So far he had said nothing, but I could see from behind that he was working himself up, shaking himself and frowning as he does on these occasions'. There followed half an hour in which 'a superb farrago of sense and sentiment, of spontaneous rhetoric and calculated art' had been deployed, in which 'he had moved himself at least as much as his audience' (JMK 10:419–20).

Then a *coup de théâtre.* A secretary rushes in and presents Lloyd George with a sealed telegram, which he duly opens and reads out with great dramatic effect, with its stark warning from the British commander on the spot of famine and civil unrest, and a demand for the immediate delivery of food supplies – 'the whole thing had been stage-managed', as Keynes discovered (JMK 10:421). Even so, one further push was needed to forestall French sabotage of an agreement, with Lloyd George now deploying banter and flattery of the French Supreme Commander, Foch, to ease him out of the picture as the final mediator and bring in a senior British admiral instead.

Only the French finance minister, Klotz, remained as an obstacle to releasing the necessary gold. 'Lloyd George had always hated him and despised him; and now saw in a twinkling that he could kill him', Keynes commented. 'Women and children were starving, he cried, and here was M. Klotz prating and prating of his "goold"'. Keynes clearly admired Lloyd George's performance, though he also saw clearly enough the passions on which he was playing. 'His eyes flashed and the words came out with a contempt so violent that he seemed almost to be spitting at him', the Memoir Club was told. 'The anti-Semitism, not far below the surface in such an assemblage as that one, was up in the heart of everyone' (JMK 10:422).

Was this wholly admirable, then, or just necessary and effective in a good cause? The nuances signalling anti-Semitism have changed a good deal in the intervening century but there is here a sense of the ends justifying the means. Clearly Keynes, no less than Lloyd George, was not fastidious about getting his hands dirty in Paris when the high issues at stake demanded it. And the final section of the memoir on Melchior discloses a positive relish for the politics of ends and means.

For Keynes was now sent on the train again, this time to Brussels, accompanying the British First Sea Lord, Admiral Rosslyn Wemyss, 'a new kind of admiral' and universally known as 'Rosie'. Keynes observed that 'with a comical, quizzical face and a single eye-glass, middle-aged, pleasure-loving, experienced and lazy, Rosie had still got a good many of the instincts of the flirtatious midshipman, and we had a very agreeable dinner in the restaurant car on that basis of relationship'. This was expressed in 'his great amusement that I, a University Professor, should, before we had finished the soup, have used the word "bloody"; he'd never before sat next to a Professor at dinner, so he said, and was greatly surprised'

(JMK 10:423–4). The young Fellow of King's had never before sat next to a Sea Lord, of course, but was unabashed.

Wemyss put up no pretence, either for Keynes or for the Germans, of having mastered any of the detail. All that mattered was that they were jointly charged with implementing the agreement reached at the Supreme War Council. 'But there was one obstacle', Keynes explained. 'The French had got their way on the point that the Germans were to give an unqualified acceptance to the surrender of the ships, before they were told of our intentions about feeding them' (JMK 10:423). Another moment, then, not only for discretion but for subterfuge. Wemyss came to Keynes's sleeping car on the train to Brussels, evidently worried that the Germans would blench at being asked to make the first move. 'D'you think you could see to it that they don't make any unnecessary trouble?' Keynes reports him as saying. 'I tumbled to his meaning, looked him in the eyes, and we both smiled'. Or so the memoir records their tacit understanding (JMK 10:425).

In Brussels, then, prior to the official meeting, Keynes slipped off to the hotel where Melchior was staying, evidently unprepared to receive visitors, with an unmade bed and an unemptied chamber-pot on the floor. In such furtive surroundings, the deal had to be struck. Keynes explained that the first agenda item that afternoon would be for German acceptance of the demand for surrender of the ships; only when this had been accepted would the food then be supplied. The memoir tells us that Melchior's face fell but that Keynes, looking him in the eye, gave the assurance 'for your own most private information I think it is desirable that you should know what will follow'. This was, of course, that revictualling would then take place. Melchior glanced from Keynes to the Royal Navy officer whom Wemyss had sent to accompany him, as the visual evidence that this was officially sanctioned, then turned back to Keynes and agreed, without any more being said. So Keynes was able to rejoin the First Sea Lord at the lunch table, with another wink and another nod – 'I fancy it will be all right this afternoon' – having secured Melchior's assurance that the deal would all fall into place, which it duly did (JMK 10:426). It was a triumph for discretion and expediency.

'Dr Melchior' was one of two memoirs to be published shortly after Keynes's death – the other was 'My Early Beliefs' (1938) – in implementation of 'an express desire in his will that these papers, and these alone of his unpublished writings, should be printed' (JMK 10:388). This suggests that Keynes had long intended his memoir on Melchior for ultimate publication, and the reasons for withholding it during his lifetime seem obvious enough. For one thing, it contained provoking sexual references, unmentionable in print at the time though suitable enough for an audience of his Bloomsbury friends on a winter evening in 1921. Similar reasons could be adduced to explain why '22 Hyde Park Gate' was not published until after the death of Virginia Woolf (and indeed of Leonard too). E. M. Forster's novel *Maurice*, portraying homosexuality sympathetically in the stern legal climate before the First World War, was not published until 1971. As with the extended version of Keynes's portrait of Lloyd George, withheld from the *Economic Consequences* in 1919, his memoir on Melchior was put away in a drawer, both of them texts capable at the time of embarrassing the remarkable rapprochement between Keynes and Lloyd George that took place during the 1920s.

***

By the spring of 1924, a return to the gold standard, which Britain had formally left in 1919, was plainly in the air. In May a committee jointly headed by Sir Austen Chamberlain and Sir John Bradbury of the Treasury had been set up to report on the issue; and when Keynes later gave evidence to it, he and McKenna were the only witnesses to advise against going back on gold, despite the Treasury's institutional commitment in favour. This is perhaps surprising in view of their earlier stern support for Treasury orthodoxy against the heretical Lloyd George – not to mention the impact of the *Economic Consequences* in identifying Keynes as Lloyd George's arch critic. But, as had already been apparent at the Genoa conference in 1922, such mutual perspectives were changing.

In May 1924, at a time when Lydia was herself in Paris, Maynard had been invited to a big, formal, diplomatic reception in London. 'At dinner I sat next but one to Lloyd George and talked to him a great deal', Maynard told Lydia. 'He praised my Nation article and approved it very much. Then he made indirect flatteries to me, saying to the lady between us – "I approve Keynes, because, whether he is right or wrong, he is always dealing with realities"' (Hill and Keynes 1989, 205). The article to which they referred had been published in the newly reconstituted Liberal weekly the *Nation*, of which Keynes was a financial as well as a political supporter, under the title 'Does Employment Need a Drastic Remedy?' Keynes's answer was now that it certainly did, in the form of public investment to supply 'the stimulus which shall initiate a cumulative prosperity' (JMK 19:223). In retrospect, none of this may seem surprising as an adumbration of an agenda that we immediately recognise as 'Keynesian'. Yet the article was in fact a response to one published a month earlier by Lloyd George, himself the real instigator of this line of argument.

It often seems natural to think of economic theory working, with suitable timelags, to influence subsequent economic policy. This is a suggestion that Keynes himself famously put forward in the closing passage of his *General Theory* in 1936. But in his own career there is suggestive evidence that his own thinking as an economist was at times crucially jolted into new courses by the example of leaders whose mastery of the pragmatic arts of politics he could not help admiring. Later, Franklin Roosevelt's New Deal was to attract Keynes's warm support, but not necessarily because FDR had become an early Keynesian; and at their first personal meeting Keynes was left unimpressed by the President's rather weak grasp of formal economics. Likewise, perhaps, we can understand Keynes's earlier readiness to pick up from Lloyd George the sort of cues that were only subsequently refined as economic concepts.

In this perspective, it may surprise us rather less than it shocked some contemporaries to find Keynes enlisting as a prominent supporter of Lloyd George's leadership of a reunited Liberal Party in the late 1920s. Asquith was now eclipsed in retirement, though on a personal level Keynes's obituary in 1928 – of a man 'who looked the part of Prime Minister as no one has since Mr Gladstone' – was warm enough (JMK 10:37). What animated Keynes's advocacy of Lloyd George's manifesto in 1929, *We Can Conquer Unemployment*, was the centrality of its proposal of a stimulus through loan-financed public works. It was a direct assault on the Treasury view that such public expenditure would simply divert scarce resources, which Keynes now called 'an argument which would be correct *if everyone were employed already*, but is only correct *on that assumption*' (JMK 19:823, italics in original). This too was published in an issue of the *Nation*, 18 May 1929, during an election campaign – only later to be elaborated as economic theory in the concept of the multiplier.

If that economic analysis was true in 1929, however, perhaps it had also been true in 1916 when the full productive capacity of the economy under the stimulus of war had yet to be mobilised. Here, it might be said, was much the same old wartime argument between Lloyd George and Keynes. But in the 1920s it had been laid to rest, in a manner that any reader of 'Dr Melchior' would have understood – tacitly and discreetly. Disinterring such quarrels suited neither man for the moment during a happy interlude of pragmatic cooperation, with Lloyd George happy to forgive, and Keynes to forget.

It was the publication of Keynes's book *Essays in Biography* in March 1933 that publicly signalled the end of the truce. At that point he decided to retrieve the half-dozen pages of his portrait of Lloyd George, 'this syren', omitted from the *Economic Consequences*. If these do not make entirely comfortable reading now, as little more than an ethnic stereotype rendered in overdrawn rhetoric, then the much greater sense of shock at the time can surely be appreciated. The press naturally seized upon this rift. Given the recent and prominent cooperation between the two men, predicated on letting bygones be bygones, a sense of resentment on Lloyd

George's part was surely to be expected – and did not wait long to find expression.

In November 1933 the first volume of Lloyd George's *War Memoirs* appeared, rehearsing the arguments between himself and the Treasury in 1915. He now denounced Keynes as 'much too mercurial and impulsive a counsellor for a great emergency' when the young man had been 'for the first time lifted by the Chancellor of the Exchequer into the rocking chair of the pundit'. In a judgement with inevitable and ironic application to their recent joint campaign on unemployment, Lloyd George concluded: 'It seems rather absurd when now not even his friends – least of all his friends – have any longer the slightest faith in his judgements on finance' (Lloyd George, *WM* 1:410).

Nor was this the end of their altercations. In further volumes of his memoirs Lloyd George was to resume his assault on this erstwhile Treasury pundit, whose wartime advice on the potential economic effects of exacting indemnities was now exposed in prejudicial terms. In this instance, Lloyd George was citing official archives in order to accuse Keynes of inspiring the estimates of the Heavenly Twins, Cunliffe and Sumner. The purported archival evidence, to which Keynes was himself denied access at the time, does not support this allegation, as is now generally accepted even by historians critical of Keynes's stance. But this did not inhibit Lloyd George in 1938 from calling his new book *The Truth about the Peace Treaties*.

He lived until 1945 but there seems to be no evidence, after 1931, that the two men ever spoke again. 'Regarded thus as a competition in personalities, I make no complaint of what, indeed, any prudent person would have expected from the subject in question', Keynes had written to *The Times* in November 1933, and he was surely justified in calling these exchanges 'perhaps as inexcusable on the one side as on the other' (JMK 30:18–19). It was only in the 1972 edition of *Essays in Biography*, as Volume Ten of the *Collected Works*, that the memoir 'Dr Melchior: A Defeated Enemy' was added to the published volume – posthumously, as Keynes himself had decided, with a degree of discretion that he did not always exercise in his own lifetime.

5

Yielding to Ramsey
Probability Revisited

'The power to become habituated to his surroundings is a marked characteristic of mankind', so the very first words of the *Economic Consequences* asserted in 1919. 'Very few of us realise with conviction the intensely unusual, unstable, complicated, unreliable, temporary nature of the economic organisation by which Western Europe has lived for the last half century' (JMK 2:1). In England, Keynes admitted, this might not yet have sunk in; hence the urgency of his report on the critical condition of continental Europe, its uncertain future now hanging in the balance. His own, almost tactile, sense of crisis and transition was conveyed in this, his second book to be published. But, as we have seen, the third book that followed in August 1921 was something totally different: his *Treatise on Probability*, its date of publication belying the fact that its animating concepts had long preceded the Great War that changed everything.

Nonetheless, Keynes's ideas about probability were now launched upon the public – or rather upon members of that tiny demographic sliver of the population who took a keen interest in such matters. In Cambridge, a first year undergraduate aged eighteen called Frank Ramsey read *Probability* on publication, with consequential effects to be assessed later in this chapter. The impact of Ramsey on Keynes's thinking is not a simple matter to determine, as is shown by a contested specialist literature, of which I take account in this chapter. But some of the issues raised have further implications that seem to me worth examining further, which I shall do in Chapter 6, this time in a broader policy context, in seeking to understand the centrality of the gold standard in Keynes's career.

A few quotations from *Probability* itself are enough to convey the flavour of the enterprise – perhaps as much in the way that issues are broached as in the detailed substantiation of any claims made. 'All propositions are true or false, but the knowledge we have of them depends on our circumstances', we are told at the outset (JMK 8:3). And since everyone has different circumstances, with necessarily different degrees of knowledge, this might suggest that probability could be called subjective; but this was not what the author wished to maintain. 'A proposition is not probable because we think it so', he explains. 'When once the facts are given which determine our knowledge, what is probable or improbable in these circumstances has been fixed objectively, and is independent of our opinion' (JMK 8:4). It is the expectation that is fixed in this way, not the outcome – which may indeed turn out in unexpected ways.

Now the fact that these are very stringent conditions to meet in practice may not be worrying in an academic work of philosophy. In *Probability* Keynes was explicit in maintaining that his immediate concern was not with 'the logic of implication and the categories of truth and falsehood' but rather with 'the logic of probability and the categories of knowledge, ignorance, and rational belief' (JMK 8:8). It might, indeed, be rational to believe what eventually turns out to be false. All this is consistent with the conclusion of his book, that 'there is no direct relation between the truth of a proposition and its probability. Probability begins and ends with probability' (JMK 8:356). Yet Keynes's concept of probability, as he insisted at this time, was objective; it was based on our perception of knowledge, albeit a degree of knowledge that was partial and thus fell short of certainty. For he insisted that an *objective* probability could be perceived, basically through intuition. It was the differing views or opinions about any matter that could be called *subjective*, and probability itself was unaffected.

Now the fact that opinion was subjective was hardly unimportant, of course, in matters of politics and economics. In Cambridge the study of these disciplines (along with philosophy) had long been considered as the province of 'the moral sciences' – this was indeed the original name of the Tripos that encompassed them. And in considering the application of his rigorous model in such contexts, Keynes dismissed the project of 'bringing the moral sciences under the sway of mathematical reasoning' as a nineteenth-century delusion (JMK 8:349). It was essentially the status of intuition that had guided him here, in asserting that a probability relationship could be perceived on the basis of partial knowledge.

In understanding why intuition was prized in this way, the influence of the Cambridge philosopher, G. E. Moore, is pivotal. It is difficult to escape the impact that he made upon the undergraduates who became Keynes's circle of friends, notably those 'Apostles' some two or three years his elder, especially Lytton Strachey, Leonard Woolf, Ralph

Hawtrey and Saxon Sydney-Turner. Strachey's inevitable vocation was as a writer; the other three Apostles mentioned here were to commence formal careers by taking the competitive examinations for entry to the civil service – like Keynes himself of course, their junior as an undergraduate but immediately recognised as one of their ilk and co-opted accordingly. 'When Maynard Keynes came up', as Woolf later put it, 'we elected him in 1903'. Moore, ten years older than Keynes, remained active in meetings of the Apostles. And Woolf was not alone in professing his sense that Moore was simply 'a great man', a conviction that was lifelong in his case. 'The intensity of Moore's passion for truth was an integral part of his greatness, and purity of passion was an integral part of his whole character' (Woolf 1960, 130, 135).

Moore's influence had serious intellectual consequences, but was not simply intellectual in origin nor in the way it was projected. His central contention, much prized by those Apostles who sat at his feet in pre-war Cambridge, was that our perception of the 'good' is essentially intuitive. Here is the basis for Anna Carabelli's pithy contention: 'Keynes's probability shared all the attributes of Moore's concept of goodness: it was a simple notion, unanalysable, indefinable, non-natural, directly perceived or intuited and objective' (Carabelli 1988, 31). Hence the young Keynes's confidence in intuition as the basis for a perception of probability that was nonetheless objective, even though it did not rely upon measurement of frequency; nor could the strength of such a belief be explained as psychological; nor could it be satisfactorily measured.

Nonetheless, when Keynes turned with relief from his long-standing task of preparing the final revision of

Probability for the publishers during 1920, he was left facing the sort of problems in which the status of opinion remained a pressing problem. Indeed this was central to what he was saying in his *Revision of the Treaty*, published only a few months later. If we were to extend his style of reasoning in *Probability* to a practical political issue, one in which there was a difference between inside opinion and outside opinion, could it justify the view that inside opinion, being based on more relevant knowledge, was therefore more likely to turn out to be true? Moreover, the likelihood that, in the world of politics, the state of opinion might itself affect the outcome was surely relevant. A popular policy might work better, simply because it was more widely acceptable to public opinion.

In this perspective, a particular example could be found in what Keynes had argued at one point in his very first book, *Indian Currency and Finance*, which seems to prefigure some of the author's later thinking about public opinion. For, already in 1913, he comments on the proposal to open an official mint for gold in India itself (as well as that in London) that the government 'would have a pleasant feeling of being democratic on an occasion when to yield involves no more evil that any other expenditure on a piece of fairly cheap ostentation' (JMK 1:62). Keynes makes it clear that this is a hypothetical argument, since he did not believe that such a democratic demand actually existed. But later in the book he takes a relaxed position on a compromise proposal:

> In deference to a public opinion which does not clearly understand the purpose of the reserves or the limitations under which the secretary of state must needs act in

managing his sterling resources, it may be worth while
to allay a groundless suspicion by the compromise of
holding a fair proportion of the reserve of actual gold coin
in India herself. (JMK 1:136)

Stressing the importance of confidence in sustaining
the market would be another, and less political, way of putting this. To this extent it could be concluded that the author's
first book already shows him adept at deploying his insider
expertise to good effect. After all, in the Cambridge school of
economics in which Keynes had been 'brought up', as he liked
to put it, the importance of confidence in governing the business cycle had long been axiomatic. Opinions mattered, true
or not; how they were formed was the crux. Indeed, such a
view seems already implicit in Keynes's thinking at the time
he wrote his *Economic Consequences*, as can be seen in its
final sentence: 'To the formation of the general opinion of the
future I dedicate this book' (JMK 2:189).

In three very different but almost contemporary
books – the *Economic Consequences*, *Probability* and his
Revision of the Treaty – Keynes was scrutinising, through different lenses, issues about our conception of truth, about the
status of our beliefs, and about our actions and their likely
consequences. The fact that such questions frame Keynes's
long-standing intellectual and moral concerns will surely
be obvious to any modern reader of *Probability*, which is
no longer just a neglected, orphan volume in the *Collected
Works*. Aptly responding to the fresh promptings in the academic literature of the 1980s, Donald Moggridge commented
in his magisterial biography of Keynes: 'The whole logic of

Probability was the logic of rational beliefs rather than of truth' (Moggridge 1992, 146).

***

In the preface to *Probability*, Keynes consigned the book 'for criticism and enlargement at the hand of others, doubtful whether I myself am likely to get much further, by waiting longer, with a work, which, beginning as a fellowship Dissertation, and interrupted by the war, has already extended over many years' (JMK 8: preface). In fulfilling this projected task, whether described as that of criticising or enlarging, one hand inescapably stands out: that of Frank Ramsey, a precociously young polymath at Cambridge whose premature death in 1930 at the age of twenty-six makes his achievements in mathematics, philosophy and economics all the more remarkable.

Ramsey had been only seventeen when he became a freshman at Trinity College, Cambridge, in 1920. His background was in many ways like that of Keynes himself: from an academic family, a father who was a Fellow of a Cambridge college, a mother, also with university education, who was active in good works and progressive causes; their boy winning a scholarship to an elite public school (Winchester) and a further scholarship to a prestigious college (Trinity). Michael Ramsey, Frank's younger brother, was subsequently to become Archbishop of Canterbury, making it a moot point as to which of their stars shines more brightly in the eyes of eternity; in their lifetime they had a warm and supportive relationship, despite religious differences. Frank was a declared atheist and also a socialist. He had read the *Economic*

Consequences as soon as it was published at the end of 1919; a cheap Labour Party edition soon followed. As Frank's left-wing undergraduate friend Kingsley Martin later put it: 'about Keynes's magnificent pamphlet everyone was agreed. I remember one Socialist complaining that the place should be called Keynesbridge' (Martin 1969, 1:102).

Frank Ramsey was admitted to Trinity College on a major scholarship in October 1920, reading for the Mathematics Tripos. Three months later he met Keynes, who invited him to join his Political Economy Club, meeting in the rooms that he occupied as a Fellow of King's on Monday evenings. It was little surprise that both Ramsey and his close friend Richard Braithwaite were elected to the Apostles in 1921. It was Braithwaite who was to edit both Ramsey's post-humous essays and (forty years on) *Probability* in Keynes's *Collected Works*. This was a tight-knit circle, privileged in more senses than one but also licensed for exchanges of sharp mutual criticism irrespective of any formal hierarchy of academic status. Both Ramsey and Braithwaite read *Probability* on its publication; in a review published in January 1922, Ramsey made clear his fundamental reservations, which were enough to shake his friend Braithwaite. The extent to which *Probability* relied on supposedly objective intuitions, much as Moore had done in sustaining his concept of the good, was not likely to have been persuasive for Ramsey, who had now dutifully attended Moore's lectures, only to find himself disappointed by their incoherence.

Despite Ramsey's sceptical review of *Probability*, Keynes nonetheless asked him to check his mathematics for him in correspondence with other critics. Indeed their friendship ripened despite a twenty-year gap in age and, for the moment, some fundamental differences on methodology that Keynes well recognised. As he noted, in a private letter, 'Ramsey and the other young men at Cambridge are quite obdurate, and still believe that *either* Probability is a definitely measurable entity, precisely connected with Frequency, *or* is of merely psychological importance and is definitely non-logical' (Bateman 1996, 63, emphasis in original). On this reading, then, there were two options, as the subsequent development of methodologies in this field has served to confirm. *Either* an objective frame for specifying the probability of a particular outcome could perhaps be salvaged via some quantitative measure of observed frequency in the past (which is essentially how statisticians normally proceed today). *Or* a concept focussed on expectations could perhaps be salvaged via an admission of some subjectivity in the formation of such prior beliefs as to what was probable (which is what modern psychological theories would suggest).

Keynes would, at this point, formally endorse neither option. He purported to stand by his own published theory, affirming the existence of prior expectations which were indeed objective because they were founded on perceptions that were valid for intuitive and self-evident reasons. But Ramsey would not go away; he was now part of Keynes's circle in Cambridge, elected with Keynes's support as a Fellow of King's in 1924. Keynes continued to rely on his help in resolving key mathematical issues and was present at five of the seven papers that Ramsey gave to the Apostles in these years, one of them, in the autumn of 1923, again questioning the faith in intuitive induction (which Keynes had imbibed from Moore). As Ramsey put the issue: 'Induction is reasonable because it produces predictions which are generally verified, not because of any logical relation between its premise and conclusion' (Misak 2020, 117). Keynes took no offence; for him Ramsey was a protégé rather than an opponent.

Yet Ramsey's most telling criticism of Keynes, in a paper finalised in 1926 called 'Truth and Probability', clearly hit home at an intellectual level. Ramsey did not make the argument about frequency, or its objective scientific measurement, into the crux of his case, deliberately putting this question aside. Instead he chose to direct attention to the logic of partial belief, which was Keynes's own chosen ground in his *Probability*.

One remarkable thing in this intellectual confrontation between two towering intellectual figures is that the issues were posed, and largely resolved, in a manner that seems almost conversational in its timbre, relying heavily on common sense and plain speaking to carry conviction. In Ramsey's paper, as published posthumously in 1931, his key point against Keynes is simply 'that there really do not seem to be any such things as the probability relations he describes'. Almost anecdotally, Ramsey adds that:

> [S]peaking for myself I feel confident that this is not true. I do not perceive them, and if I am to be persuaded that they exist it must be by argument; moreover I shrewdly suspect that others do not perceive them either, because they are able to come to so very little agreement as to which of them relates any two given propositions. (Ramsey 1931, 161)

Ramsey thus appealed, in these subjective terms, to the importance of subjectivism itself. It was an appeal to bring 'human logic or the logic of truth' into the picture, rather than Keynes's epic task in the five hundred pages of *Probability* of mounting an argument within the formal logic of objective science. And Keynes's response was equally remarkable, given the stake that any academic would have in justifying the results of some fifteen years of (admittedly intermittent) scholarly scrutiny of such a topic. Yet I think Robert Skidelsky justified in commenting on the impact of Ramsey's critique that 'little of the baroque edifice of the *Treatise* was left standing' (Skidelsky 1992, 70). If the perception of a degree of objective truth is via intuition (as Keynes had wished to maintain) the problem is surely that such a perception (however much prized by ourselves) may be compromised – or may have no foundation. Hence Keynes's vulnerability to Ramsey's blunt assertion that he personally had no such faculty of perception. It was only a matter of time before Keynes capitulated.

***

If, for the moment, Keynes offered no formal written response to Ramsey, it can surely be pleaded that he was busy enough with other matters in the 1920s. He had become, as we have seen, deeply engaged in journalism; and he was currently formulating controversial views on economic policy, often in support of Lloyd George, faced with the problem of mounting unemployment in Britain. Keynes could even be called a minor press baron himself now, with his acquisition of a controlling interest in the *Nation*, a left-wing Liberal weekly (in which he installed his Cambridge colleague Hubert Henderson as editor, with Leonard Woolf as literary editor). The forum of the Liberal Summer Schools, in which Keynes became active, also served to propagate his ideas, with lectures like 'Am I a Liberal?' republished in the *Nation*, and later collected with like-minded polemical pieces in the volume *Essays in Persuasion* (1931) (now expanded further as JMK 7).

All this took time, energy, mental engagement in the task of the moment, often against an unforgiving deadline when a pamphlet or an article for the newspapers had to go to press. One way or another, it does not seem necessary to suppose that, in these years, Keynes entertained *any* strict, formal theory of probability, baroque or otherwise. Rescuing the theoretical foundation of his epistemology had yielded to more pressing concerns, not only in public policy but also in economic analysis.

For Keynes also now set himself the further task of theorising his position as an economist in a second big Treatise – the two volumes of his *Treatise on Money* (1929), which can hardly be ignored in any survey of his thinking in the late 1920s. Its publication, often delayed while the author tried to square its evolving text with the latest brainwave generated by his polemical engagements, was a major step in his academic career, cementing an oeuvre that otherwise might have been satirised as crazy paving. The fundamental analysis of the *Treatise on Money* was concerned primarily with the hydraulic flows that sought to equilibrate the system, with special attention to the relationship between interest rates and the gold standard. In his analysis, Keynes acknowledged the contribution of his Cambridge colleague Dennis Robertson, with whom he had extensive correspondence, leading to much revision of the original text.

In one striking passage, added at a late stage in the chapter 'Historical Illustrations', Keynes began with a revealing comment on his own methodology, suggesting that, instead of applying it to hypothetical cases, it would be better to consider examples in the history of prices. This was how he illustrated the distinction, central to the analysis of the *Treatise on Money*, between saving and investment. 'It has been usual to think of the accumulated wealth of the world as having been painfully built up out of that voluntary abstinence of individuals from the immediate enjoyment of consumption which we call thrift', he suggested. 'But it should be obvious that mere abstinence is not enough by itself to build cities or drain fens'. Instead, another economic factor was at work – 'It is enterprise which builds and improves the world's possessions'. And this set up the essential polarity: 'If enterprise is afoot, wealth accumulates whatever may be happening to thrift; and if enterprise is asleep, wealth decays whatever thrift may be doing' (JMK 6:132).

In order to simulate enterprise, there needed to be an expectation of profit but also, crucially, access to the necessary resources to put projects into execution in the form of actual investment. Hence the importance of interest rates in establishing an equilibrium between what savers would accept and what entrepreneurs could afford, if they were to make a profit. The equilibrating role of Bank rate (to apply the British term) was thus crucial, with cheap money able to fuel an investment boom, with some inflationary effect; and conversely dear money prone to bring an economic downturn, with overall deflationary consequences. Keynes's historical examples pointed to the advantages of a mild profit inflation in increasing national wealth. Incidentally, he made one reference to Ramsey who – in an article that Keynes had accepted as editor of the *Economic Journal* – had argued for a higher rate of present accumulation to safeguard future generations (the origin of a concept of 'Ramsey Rule', only later rediscovered). But Keynes affirmed his own 'preference for a policy today which, whilst avoiding deflation at all costs, aims at the stability of purchasing power as its ideal objective' (JMK 6:144–5).

The whole analysis of the *Treatise on Money* pointed to the crucial task of interest rates in engineering an equilibrium. If the rate was set too high, savers might indeed benefit but investors would be inhibited, with consequent unemployment in a deflationary spiral downwards. Hence the rationale for the sort of shock through a 'drastic remedy' that Keynes had followed Lloyd George's lead in advocating since 1924, with a vision of cumulative prosperity stimulated through government intervention. Rather than analysing economic motivation in psychological terms, the *Treatise on Money* did little more than scatter a few tantalising hints. 'The ignorance of even the best-informed investor about the more remote future is much greater than his knowledge', we are told at one point; and we are advised that 'it may often profit the wisest to anticipate mob psychology rather than the real trend of events, and to ape unreason proleptically' (JMK 6:323). With hindsight, we might say that such suggestive remarks had to wait for the *General Theory*, as drafted by Keynes several years later, to receive his more sustained attention.

It should be said that the *Treatise on Money* secured Keynes's professional pre-eminence on both sides of the Atlantic. If we look at a citations index, compiling references to the names of macro-economists by their peers in economic journals, we find that Keynes, for all his acknowledged brilliance, had been ranked tenth in the 1920s, well behind his senior Cambridge colleagues Alfred Marshall or A. C. Pigou or the American Irving Fisher, and level-pegging with both the slightly older Ralph Hawtrey and with Dennis Robertson, seven years younger. After the *Treatise on Money*, a similar index for the early 1930s puts the name of Keynes ahead of the field internationally, with Robertson now second and Friedrich von Hayek edging Hawtrey and Fisher out of fourth place (Deutscher 1990, 189–90). Here was academic recognition to match popular fame.

***

What the author confided to his mother, however, at the time when he sent off his *Treatise on Money* for publication, suggests his own misgivings. 'This evening, at last, I have finished my book', he told her in September 1930. 'It has occupied me seven years off and on, – and so one parts from it with mixed feelings. A relief anyhow that it hasn't dragged on into next term. Artistically it is a failure – I have changed my mind too much during the course of it for it to be a proper unity' (JMK 13:176). True, a case can be made for Bradley Bateman's view that this indeed represented failure of a kind: 'Two treatises, 21 years of work, and still nothing matching the definitive status conveyed by the word *treatise*' (Bateman 1996, 68).

Such was Keynes's status, and his state of mind, at the beginning of the Cambridge Michaelmas Term, 1930, during which his *Treatise on Money* was published on 31 October. Within weeks, the local news was that Frank Ramsey had contracted jaundice; and in January 1931 the illness took a fatal turn. It was Ramsey's shocking death and the publication of his posthumous papers, edited by Braithwaite later in the same year, that finally prompted Keynes into publishing his own tribute, commending Ramsey's 'common sense and a sort of hard-headed practicality towards the whole business'. This was written for the newly amalgamated, left-wing, weekly paper *The New Statesman and Nation*, which Keynes supported financially as well as intellectually, serving as chairman of its board. It was thus an appropriate site for the obituary, especially since its new editor was Ramsey's friend Kingsley Martin. It was now that Keynes succinctly acknowledged how far he himself had moved in his thinking:

> Thus the calculus of probabilities belongs to formal logic. But the basis of our degrees of belief – or the *a priori* probabilities, as they used to be called – is part of our human outfit, perhaps given us merely by natural selection, analogous to our perceptions and our memories rather than to formal logic. So far I yield to Ramsey – I think he is right. (JMK 10:339)

And if Ramsey was right on this, the validity of our perceptions was not a self-evident matter – certainly not in fields where different people could form very different judgements and hold very different beliefs. Were these subjective probabilities, then, susceptible of measurement by some alternative methodology? 'The old-established way of measuring a person's belief is to propose a bet, and see what are the lowest odds which he will accept', Ramsey had suggested, in his homely manner (Ramsey 1931, 170). This too proved to be an influential line of future academic inquiry, with 'betting-quotients' as a measure of the strength of prospective beliefs but not, as any encounter with a racecourse bookie could affirm, offering any sort of guarantee that your horse was a sure thing to win.

The shift that took place in Keynes's epistemological views during the inter-war years has now been documented with cumulatively impressive academic authority. The implications for the development of his economic theory have understandably been to the fore. Even here it may well be the case that Keynes's unspoken assumptions governed his views – a proposition that is obviously difficult to prove by direct citation. But I think we have license to suppose that he now relaxed his view on probability, not least in the light of his newly declared agnosticism about the relation of intuition to formal proof. For example, Keynes said in one of his university lectures in April 1932, only six months after his tribute to Ramsey had been published: 'Thus theoretical economics often has a formal appearance where the reality is not strictly formal. It is not, and is not meant to be, logically watertight in the sense in which mathematics is' (JMK 29:37–8). The role played by subjective perceptions, both in guiding economic behaviour and in understanding it, was now plainly an open question.

6

Yielding to Realities
Golden Rules?

Keynes's changing view of probability, often turning on highly technical issues, can be put in a broader perspective. It surely reflected his more general abandonment of the tight, prescriptive, rules-based outlook in which he had been brought up. Responding to a changing context in turbulent times, he shifted to a more empirical approach that subsequently informed his view of economic theory and policy alike. And nowhere was this manifested more clearly than in his changing attitude towards the gold standard. Here was a central theme in his career over three decades: from the era of his first book, *Indian Currency and Finance* (1913), to his work as one of the architects of the international financial system that was instituted following the agreements reached at the Bretton Woods conference in 1944.

To anticipate, we can find a key polarity enunciated in what Keynes was to suggest in December 1941, when he turned his mind to the problem of devising feasible proposals for regulating international currencies, now looking ahead to a time when this appalling Second World War came to an end. 'Perhaps the most difficult question to determine, is how much to decide by rule and how much by discretion', Keynes wrote. 'If rule prevails, the scheme can be made more watertight theoretically. If discretion prevails, it may work better in practice' (JMK 25:73). This was, he now suggested, a tension that had become evident in the inter-war debate over the international gold standard: a system of which he had been a staunch defender as a young Treasury-minded pundit but of which he subsequently became the arch-critic.

The gold standard thus stood as a prime historical monument to an ostensibly rules-based financial system. True, there was a natural affinity with two other hallowed doctrinal commitments: that free trade was the concomitant of an international gold standard in external policy, and that the national budget must always be balanced. Here was a holy trinity of verities that had been established in Britain since the time of Gladstone, the revered Prime Minister and Chancellor of the Exchequer who, from the 1850s to the 1890s, had not only held both posts intermittently but sometimes held both together. And these verities, I suggest, depended less upon economic theory than upon the heavily moralised maxims of a particular kind of Gladstonian 'common sense' (Clarke 2015, 18–25). This was the orthodoxy upon which the financial authorities in Britain – the Treasury, working with Bank of England – faithfully sought to base their policies in the era in which Keynes came to maturity in Harvey Road.

Thus the point about the gold standard was that it purported to be a universal system, freely operating through the central banks of all countries on gold, which regulated their own reserves of bullion via changes in interest rates. If the balance of payments went down, the interest rate went up, and the hot money flowed in, propping up the reserves. In practice, much of this worked by anticipation – before 1914 very little gold had actually moved around the world.

As most economic historians put it today, it needed a hegemonic nation (which would by definition be in surplus on its international transactions) to enforce what became known as 'the rules of the game'. So all animals were equal but some were more equal than others. All were in principle open to multilateral trade, ideally on a free trade basis, though the system still worked even when tariffs were applied, albeit distorting or adjusting the terms of trade. Until the First World War, as Keynes came to realise, this system was virtually synonymous with the unique ascendancy in that era of the British Empire, which extended to no less than a quarter of the world's land mass and a quarter of global population. This was an imperialism of free trade, unlike the conventional association of European imperialism with a closed system of tariffs, promoting and protecting bilateral trade between a metropolitan country and its colonies.

It was the use to which the surpluses were put that really mattered. In 1913 Keynes had scornfully dismissed 'incitements against malevolent financiers' and commented with some condescension on the Indian penchant for hoarding gold: 'India must be allowed, I suppose, to hug her sterile favourite'. This contrasted unfavourably with 'the notorious fact that that the Bank of England holds less gold than the central bank of any other first-class Power' (JMK 1:126). One reason was that members of the British public did not generally hoard gold, nor did they need to do so in their ordinary business. Moreover, in external transactions, the Bank held these remarkably low levels of actual gold reserves because it was in effect putting them to active use rather than letting the bullion stack up in its vaults. The effect was to recycle its surpluses through the banking system, financing international investment, not only in the Empire but in other still underdeveloped countries – such as the United States in the nineteenth century.

If Keynes became the arch-critic, it was of a system that he had known as an untroubled believer. In a famous passage at the beginning of the *Economic Consequences* he evoked the pre-war world-view as it must have looked from a window in Bloomsbury.

> The inhabitant of London could order by telephone, sipping his morning tea in bed, the various products of the whole earth, in such quantity as he might see fit, and reasonably expect their early delivery upon his doorstep; he could at the same moment and by the same means adventure his wealth in the natural resources and new enterprises of any quarter of the world, and share, without exertion or even trouble, in their prospective fruits and advantages. (JMK 2:6)

Nor was this simply a factitious nostalgic view, as *Indian Currency and Finance* (1913) sufficiently illustrates. On its first page Keynes offers a brief description of the great currency reform imposed upon India in 1893 with the dismissive words that 'few are now found who dispute on broad grounds the wisdom of the change from a silver to a gold standard' (JMK 1:1). The author acknowledges the different positions of creditor countries (like Britain) and debtor countries (like India) but with the complacent comment that in the London market 'the "bank rate" policy for regulating the outflow of gold has been admirably successful in this country' (JMK 1:3).

He seeks to distinguish a simple historic reliance on gold as a country's internal currency from a 'gold-exchange standard' where the actual means of exchange used internally might be otherwise – silver, or paper money, or cheques. 'Gold is an international, but not a local currency' (JMK 1:21).

Hence the advice that Keynes gave, when summoned to the Treasury on the outbreak of war in 1914, leading Lloyd George to print Treasury bills ('pound notes') for internal circulation in the United Kingdom instead of relying on gold sovereigns. This was consistent with what Keynes had previously argued, that if gold reserves leaked away into circulation as currency, this put a government 'in a weaker position to meet a crisis than if they are concentrated in its own chests' (JMK 1:65). The crucial point was that official gold reserves were meant to be used, not hoarded. In the peculiar situation of August 1914 – a sudden crisis, a need for immediate action, an initially uninstructed Chancellor – Keynes's advice became adopted as government policy, not only on issuing paper money for domestic use but also on a second count. In his eyes, it was consistent to maintain that the British government, with its own chests now full, should *not* freeze its international gold reserves. Instead, specie payment should be honoured. Moreover, the behaviour of the high-street banks in already refusing to pay out gold to their domestic customers, thus making them queue up at the Bank of England instead, was termed a 'shameful sight' by Keynes, readily resorting here to the language of moral repugnance (JMK 11:254).

The Bank of England itself continued to pay out gold, abroad if not at home; specie payment was maintained externally, while paper currency was printed by the Treasury for internal circulation. So Britain, unlike almost every other

141

country, did not lock up its own international gold reserves in this crisis. Hence Keynes's proud, patriotic, public boast: 'The Bank of England alone met the international catastrophes of August, 1914, without suspending specie payments and without availing herself of emergency privileges' (JMK 11:278). In his eyes at the time, 'the vital point is that we should not repudiate our external obligations to pay gold, until it is physically impossible for us to fulfil them' (JMK 16:13).

Keynes, soon himself a Treasury official with responsibility for Britain's external payments, maintained this position throughout the war. A memorandum written in January 1917, before the United States became a belligerent, conveys his steadfast moral commitment at that time to maintaining Britain's stance. 'In the past we have made a fetish of the gold standard', he wrote – and with full approval. 'We have taken immense pride in it and constantly proclaimed to the world that it is the cornerstone of our policy'. He still insisted that this was correct, above all in maintaining confidence. To abandon gold, he suggested, 'is gravely injurious to our credit; and it affords encouragement to the enemy'. Moreover, he concluded his case against Britain going off gold with the remarkable words: 'It is not so much a possible policy for deliberate adoption, as the symptom, if it occurs, of a grave disease' (JMK 16:222). These are hardly economic arguments for the expediency of one policy option as against another. They surely suggest a much deeper moral commitment to sticking by the rules as a matter of honour in playing the game.

We might pause at this point to ask a more general question: did Keynes always insist that it was right to obey general rules? It is an issue that has been much debated, not least because of what he wrote himself, with beguiling but misleading literary artifice, in his memoir 'My Early Beliefs'. Like 'Dr Melchior', this had been composed for the Memoir Club, and likewise kept discreetly unpublished until after Keynes's death; so it is subject to all the usual caveats about how far it should be taken literally. In fact, as we have seen, his own philosophical position was highly sophisticated, especially about probability. Still influenced by Moore, the young Keynes had confronted the issue of 'rules' by acknowledging their general social utility but differed from Moore in claiming a right to personal judgement, licensed on the grounds of conscience. And Keynes's own refusal on principle to submit to military conscription in 1916 had been argued on this moral basis. He was thus indeed a conscientious objector – but not objecting (as a pacifist might have done) to military service in itself, only to the use of conscription to enforce the rule.

This is surely a pertinent point in questioning the scope and ambit of a rules-based morality, and asserting an individual right to dissent or to exercise discretion. Yet in 1917, only a year after he had (albeit unnecessarily) claimed conscientious objection, but now writing with his Treasury hat on, Keynes seemed to grant rules some higher kind of legitimacy when applied to the gold standard. Admittedly, participation in the gold standard could be considered different because it was optional; only the members who have chosen to join a club are bound by its rules. But opting to resign from a club is not normally described as the symptom of a grave disease.

***

The legitimacy of rules surely rests on an implicit assumption that the rules are fair, and that they bear equally and equitably upon all the parties concerned. At what point the gold standard failed to meet this test in Keynes's eyes is perhaps the real question. It is surely relevant here that in 1919 the *Economic Consequences* spoke to his sense of the organic interdependence of all the European countries, rather than fallaciously supposing them as engaged in a zero-sum game between winners and losers (Carabelli and Cedrini 2014, 101–2, 107). And there is copious evidence in Keynes's writings from the Genoa conference in 1921, and in the *Manchester Guardian* supplements, of him adopting such a perspective.

What he had urged at Genoa started from the premise that the key issue was stabilisation of currencies. 'Hitherto only one good solution has been found, a world-wide gold standard', he argued in the *Manchester Guardian* (20 April 1922), with the conclusion: 'I see no other solution of stabilization practicable now, except this traditional solution – namely a gold standard in as many countries as possible'. Yet the trouble was that this traditional objective had currently become entangled with the objective of 'improving or appreciating the exchanges (from the point of view of the particular country), or, as it is now often called, the problem of deflation' (JMK 17:356).

Here was the serpent that, in Keynes's eyes, lay in wait to poison all post-war attempts to return to the Garden of Eden. It meant that, while 'stabilisation' was now 'the popular cry (that is to say, the word on the lips of Prime Ministers and journalists)', it was 'not at all what the governors of the state banks of Europe are taking as their ideal', which was the largely undeclared objective of deflation (JMK 17:357). This sounded very much like a division within 'inside opinion' rather than a direct clash with 'outside opinion'. Under the banner of 'stabilisation', then, Keynes now promoted a campaign against the central bankers. Almost inevitably, he lost his battle at Genoa; but his war on deflation was to define his outlook and his public stance for the rest of his life.

These concerns can indeed be termed cosmopolitan rather than nationalistic. But it should not be forgotten – Keynes himself was keenly aware of this – that, in economic terms, Britain was among the losers in the post-war world. In surrendering its long-run financial supremacy as a creditor country to the United States, Britain lost its pre-1914 status within this system, when in effect it had been able to impose British prices upon the whole world. This had always seemed so effortless – at least, to well-placed bankers in London, or to elite Treasury officials, or even to Cambridge dons, sipping their morning tea in bed. When Britain returned to the gold standard in 1925, it did so in a weaker position than hitherto: as a country that, in the end, had to obey the rules as interpreted by the only country that could now call the shots.

Keynes had commented on the significance of this rise of American financial power a couple of years previously in his *Tract on Monetary Reform*. In his eyes, by hoarding gold inflows instead of stemming them by lowering interest rates, the newly empowered United States was not behaving with the enlightened benevolence that he had too easily imputed to Great Britain in the past. 'For the past two years, the United States has *pretended* to maintain a gold standard', he asserted in 1924.

> *In fact* it has established a dollar standard; and, instead
> of ensuring that the value of the dollar shall conform to
> that of gold, it makes provision, at great expense, that the
> value of gold shall conform to that of the dollar. This is
> the way by which a rich country is able to combine new
> wisdom with old prejudice. (JMK 4:155, italics in original)

For Keynes, this came as a practical illustration of the crucial theoretical flaw in the whole ethos of the gold standard. Its Gladstonian status had been as an inexorably impartial moderator of the world system, proof against all meddling influences, on the hallowed argument that 'since governing authorities lack wisdom as often as not, a managed currency will, sooner or later, come to grief' (JMK 4:132). This was indeed the traditional dichotomy. 'But the war has effected a great change', Keynes now argued. 'Gold itself has become a "managed" currency'. The behaviour of the United States simply exemplified this. There was no 'ready-made standard' and thus 'in the modern world of paper currency and bank credit there is no escape from a "managed" currency, whether we wish it or not'. Step by step, driven mainly by a transatlantic example that offended his British susceptibilities, Keynes built up to his sweeping theoretical conclusion: 'In truth the gold standard is already a barbarous relic' (JMK 4:134–8).

This foreshadowed Keynes's own practical advice in 1925 to the newly appointed Chancellor of the Exchequer, Winston Churchill, not to return to the gold standard at the pre-war parity of $4.86. Churchill duly listened; he challenged his Treasury officials and the Bank of England to respond on behalf of 'the authorities'; but in the end he followed their duly authoritative advice; and he was subsequently to call it his greatest mistake. He may have been overborne and out-faced by the authorities, especially by the taciturn presence of the Governor of the Bank of England, Montagu Norman – against whom Churchill subsequently nourished a grudge. But some hint as to who had the better of the argument per-meates a comment that the Chancellor made in the House of Commons, that Keynes was 'a master of every aspect of this question, and discusses it with the utmost fluency and effectiveness upon all occasions, seasonable and unseasonable alike' (Clarke 1993, 91).

In this Churchill was somewhat like Lloyd George, whose acknowledgement that Keynes was 'always dealing with realities' captures the sense that he broached relevant insights about a fast-changing world, rather than simply mouthing the verities that still held sway in the Treasury or the Bank of England. Though Britain was now finding itself unable to play its hegemonic role any more, a candid appreci-ation of the new reality was delayed. As Keynes put it, in writ-ing to one of the Directors of the Bank: 'The more I spend my thoughts on these matters, the more alarmed do I become at seeing you and the others in authority attacking the problems of the changed post-war world with – I know you will excuse my saying so – unmodified pre-war views and ideas' (JMK 19:271–2). Not for the last time, a popular illusion persisted that Britain remained more powerful and autonomous than was actually the case.

As Keynes's career illustrates, his economic insights were often generated by real-world problems that he saw around him. Reparations had become one such issue, making Keynes famous – but in a way that was far from 'Keynesian', as we now understand that label. In the *Economic Consequences* the analysis of reparations is often presented in terms that the author of the *General Theory* would subsequently have labelled 'classical' in its tight framework of analysis; it was thus 'Ricardian' in its assumption that all consequences can be offset by exactly equivalent future effects within the same system of accounting. Thus Keynes's polemical insistence that it was impossible for Germany to pay the levels of reparations demanded in the Treaty had helped generate interest in the highly academic 'transfer problem'. A famous debate between himself and the Swedish economist Bertil Ohlin was to bring this to a head in 1929. Now Ohlin's thinking was, in a sense, more 'Keynesian' than that of Keynes himself at this point, as his focus on the possible effects of transfers in stimulating aggregate demand immediately suggests to us today. It was Keynes who proved slow to recognise the full implications of Ohlin's point, only saying that 'if Germany succeeds in making reparation payments, this will set up a new situation with a repercussion which may indirectly benefit Germany' (JMK 11:472). The potency of such potential 'multiplier' effects had yet to find their champions; it was still Keynes who adopted 'an extremely classical view' in this controversy (Gomes 2010, 228–32).

The gold standard itself became another and more direct object lesson for Keynes. With sterling now back on gold, British prices in future had to follow the dollar. It was with a rueful awareness that this was now the American century that Keynes subsequently looked – with a new scepticism – on the rules of the international gold standard. His pamphlet 'The Economic Consequences of Mr Churchill' (1925) famously forged the link between Britain's return to gold and the problem of unemployment. Keynes now argued that the parity of the currency should be set by internal conditions – to reflect British prices in sterling at home – rather than imposed externally through an inflexible parity as required by adherence to the gold standard, which left internal prices to adjust accordingly through deflation. As he put it during his debate with Ohlin, the difficulty lay in 'applying the theory of liquids to what is, if not a solid, at least a sticky mass with strong internal resistances' (JMK 11:458).

Keynes thus expressed his disillusionment with a system that merely purported to be simultaneously *neutral* in its impact on each participating country and *benign* in its capacity to foster the prosperity of all. He had now plainly ceased to invest the gold standard and financial orthodoxy with any higher claims. Indeed as early as 1923 he had written scathingly that 'many conservative bankers regard it as more consonant with their cloth, and also as economising thought, to shift public discussion of financial topics off the logical on to an alleged "moral" plane, which means a realm of thought where vested interest can be triumphant over the common good without further debate' (JMK 4:57).

Keynes's political philosophy thus came to offer an explicit repudiation of many prevalent assumptions. In 1926 his friends Leonard and Virginia Woolf were happy to print his pamphlet, 'The End of Laissez-Faire', at their new Hogarth Press. 'The world is *not* so governed from above that private and social interests always coincide', Keynes now wrote. 'It is *not* so managed here below that in practice they coincide. It is *not* a correct deduction from the principles of economics that enlightened self-interest always operates in the public interest' (JMK 9:287–8). But this simply set the parameters for the pragmatic task of reforming the market system. 'For my part I think that capitalism, wisely managed, can probably be made more efficient for attaining economic ends than any alternative system yet in sight, but that in itself it is in many ways extremely objectionable' (JMK 9:294).

***

One of the essential virtues claimed for the gold standard was the priority of rules, understood in a sense that Keynes himself helped to establish. Here is what he wrote in 'The Economic Consequences of Mr Churchill':

> The Bank of England is *compelled* to curtail credit by all the rules of the gold standard game. It is acting conscientiously and 'soundly' in doing so. But this does not alter the fact that to keep a tight hold on credit – and no one will deny that the Bank is doing that – necessarily involves intensifying unemployment in the present circumstances of this country. … Deflation does not reduce wages 'automatically'. It reduces them by causing unemployment. (JMK 9:220, italics in original)

We see here a very different view of the gold standard from that taken by Keynes in his Treasury years, and one identifying three salient features. First, then, it was a country fearing a deficit that *had* to act; it was a country enjoying a surplus that could *choose* to act. This is fundamental. A creditor country might choose to act as a good neighbour, following a course of enlightened self-interest that fostered tendencies to expansion; or it might not, thus forcing any debtor country into measures that entailed contraction. Seen through Keynes's British spectacles, it often seemed that Britain had duly fulfilled its previous hegemonic role in its days of power whereas the United States had inherited the power but chose not to fulfil the responsibilities. Secondly, the supposed automacity of a rules-based system in achieving necessary adjustments is challenged by Keynes's stark identification of the actual impact of the mechanisms involved. Thirdly, Keynes points to both the social inequity and to the economic inefficiency of this process.

The coal industry was the prime example. If British coal were to be exported as previously, it would now have to be at American prices, set at $4.86 to the pound, thus lower in sterling prices at the new exchange rate – and thus in turn requiring wage cuts. 'The gold standard, with its dependence on pure chance, its faith in "automatic adjustments", and its general regardlessness of social detail, is an essential emblem and idol of those who sit in the top tier of the machine' (JMK 9:224). So these were rules that inflicted heavy penalties. Yet they had to be accepted by a debtor country – or in Britain's case a country now suddenly fearing the loss of its customary surplus on the balance of payments. And the consequent dear-money policy came at a cost to social equity of which the privileged classes seemed unconscious. This pamphlet of 1925 seems to be the origin of the usage 'rules of the game' as applied to the gold standard, notably in the sense of an obligation on a creditor country not to hoard gold surpluses but to recycle them (through foreign investment).

The term's usage was reinforced by Keynes's own evidence, given while his *Treatise on Money* was in the press, to a government inquiry, the Macmillan Committee on Finance and Industry, of which he had been appointed a member by the new (minority) Labour government in October 1929. Here was a forum in which he found supportive allies not only in Reginald McKenna, his old boss at the Treasury and now a banker, but also in Ernest Bevin, the forceful leader of the Transport and General Workers' Union. And here was the opportunity not only for cross-questioning the inevitable representatives of financial orthodoxy in the Treasury and the Bank of England, but also for Keynes to supply an exposition of his own analysis.

Invited to give evidence himself over several days in February 1930, Keynes took the pre-publication proofs of his forthcoming *Treatise* as his text (and amended some parts of them in the process). 'You so conduct your affairs that you tend neither to gain not to lose large quantities of gold', was how the author glossed 'the rules of the game' (JMK 20:42). He was now permitted, in effect, to lead the Macmillan Committee through an informal seminar on how the gold standard actually operated. His exposition became canonical. The leading orthodox economist on the committee (Professor Theodore Gregory) simply added: 'I accept everything that Mr Keynes has said, but I should like to emphasise that this is not only a beautiful series of assumptions, but assumptions which translated into action have worked' (JMK 20:54).

Whether they had in fact worked, at least for Britain since it returned to gold in 1925, was really the point. The authorities pointed to the importance of adjustments being made; the facts pointed to a 'stickiness' that showed British wages failing to follow the downward path demanded by the pound sterling now being set at $4.86. Here was a gap, not least in credibility, with few explanations forthcoming. When the inscrutable Montagu Norman was subsequently brought to testify on behalf of the Bank of England, he confessed that 'it is a curious thing, the extent to which many of those who inhabit the City of London find difficulty in stating the reasons for the faith that is in them' (Clarke 1988, 140). Like his notable predecessor, Cunliffe of 'the Heavenly Twins', the Governor simply tapped his nose when pressed for answers.

The problem had been to bring down British prices; and nobody questioned Keynes's statement that 'the essence of our actual situation is that you have no corrective other than Bank rate' (JMK 20:43). The next step was inexorable. 'There is no way by which Bank rate brings down prices except through the increase of unemployment', Keynes explained. 'It brings down prices by causing enterprises to sell at a loss, but it does not bring them down to the equilibrium price level except by operating through unemployment'. This process was 'of the essence of the classical theory which, as I say, no one would deny before the War', he argued; and he himself met no denial now in expounding this historic doctrine (JMK 20:49–51). 'You see what a very good doctrine it is', Keynes claimed, somewhat archly, 'because the completely harmonious disposition of the economic forces of the world is preserved merely by the Bank of England changing the Bank rate from time to time in an appropriate way and leaving all the rest to the operation of *laissez faire*' (JMK 20:53).

And had it done the trick, here and now, since 1925? Manifestly not. There was no dissent when Keynes said that Britain was now further off equilibrium after five years of the prescribed medicine. 'I would not put forward the United States as the main criminal, except for short periods', he said. 'It was, really, the return to the gold standard in many other countries which caused them to behave just as we have; they were struggling to deflate. That is the root cause of the situation' (JMK 20:57). It was also the reason that the *Treatise* was able to present a 'special case' for action, since 'there remains in reserve a weapon by which a country can partially rescue itself when its international disequilibrium is involving it in severe unemployment'. And this, of course, was that 'the Government must itself promote a programme of domestic investment' (JMK 6:337).

The *Treatise on Money*, as published in October 1930, was to devote three of its four concluding chapters to the problem of the international management of money. Describing the gold standard as 'part of the apparatus of conservatism', Keynes sought to sketch an alternative – yet pragmatically conceded that this might be best achieved by incremental steps, including an ongoing role for gold (JMK 6:268). In this way he justified reviving ideas that he had first floated at the Genoa conference: to urge that 'the best practical objective might be the management of the value of gold by a supernational authority', leaving national monetary systems 'each with a discretion to vary the value of its local money in terms of gold within a range of (say) 2 per cent' (JMK 6:303).

Keynes currently held both the United States and France culpable, as he made clear elsewhere in late 1930. 'Their unwillingness to lend internationally, which is at the root of the trouble, is not directly due to gold', he commented, meaning that they did not have to abstain in this way; but if they chose to do so, the results were certainly bad. In a competitive race to the bottom, there were thus no winners, just a reinforcement of the contractionary forces endemic in the system itself: the many losers unable to act otherwise by themselves. 'Therefore it seems to me one needs for the solution of the problem some sort of international policy by an international institution towards international lending – something a little remote from the gold problem' (JMK 30:15). Tentatively but suggestively, he now spoke of a need 'for the creditor countries to see if they could not get together in some way to break the vicious circle, because it is a vicious circle – the less we lend the more insolvent the would-be borrower countries become' (JMK 30:17).

Keynes did not have modern economic terminology about 'policy space' or 'policy independence' at his disposal in 1930; but I do not think it is anachronistic to infer that he was already thinking of a successful international system as 'one which establishes its "rules of the game" on the need to enlarge, rather than restrict, national autonomy and policy space' (Carabelli and Cedrini 2010, 320). And this the gold standard now failed to do. Its failure was most dramatically signalled in the 1930s by the successive abandonment of gold by Britain in 1931 and by the United States in 1933 – first by the old and then by the new hegemonic power in the functioning of this system.

As the newly inaugurated President Roosevelt put it, it was time to reject the 'old fetishes of the so-called international bankers'. Many Europeans, hearing this, were shocked and disapproving; so in hailing Roosevelt as 'magnificently right', Keynes found himself a lonely voice in commending the rationality of this step. 'The Treasury and the Bank of England have depended on their sense of smell alone', he wrote, in a knowing dig at more than one governor of the Bank of England (JMK 21:273–5). Perhaps he meant that they had only used their discretion in order to follow the wrong rules, and were then forced to dissimulate about the consequences.

For until the eve of the Second World War, the authorities in Britain, unlike the United States, continued to pretend that they had been forced off the gold standard and were eager to return to it. It was a story that failed to impress the economists of the League of Nations in 1938, since in practice it was obvious how much Britain benefited from its new ability to keep the exchange rate of sterling low enough to permit (if not to stimulate) domestic recovery (Clavin 2013, 214). The official line was still that the authorities abhorred having to exercise such discretion and simply pined for the old rules of the game to be reinstated. The British government was able, for the moment, to enjoy the luxury of such hypocrisy.

In retrospect, Keynes confidently identified a fundamental inequity: that following the rules was in fact an *option* for the strong but a *necessity* for the weak in settling international payments. He claimed in 1941 that there had been 'only two periods of about fifty years each (the ages of Elizabeth and Victoria in English chronology) when the use of money for the conduct of international trade can be said to have "worked"' – and for reasons that, in retrospect, appeared fortuitous. 'To suppose that there exists some smoothly functioning automatic mechanism of adjustment which preserves equilibrium if only we trust to methods of *laissez-faire* is a doctrinaire delusion which disregards the lessons of historical experience without having behind it the support of sound theory' (JMK 25:21–2). Keynes's quest was now to reconcile pragmatic experience with theoretical insights in a rapidly changing world.

7

Truths between Friends
Cambridge and Economics

Maynard and Lydia had been able to marry in 1925, and to set up home together in Gordon Square, only after many protracted difficulties. One of these had concerned Lydia's marital status since divorce from her previous husband was complicated by the fact that he was himself a bigamist; but Maynard, nothing if not an ingenious problem-solver, eventually got that settled. He also successfully introduced Lydia to Harvey Road; his mother Florence became a champion of their liaison; and his brother Geoffrey likewise found that it eased his own relations with Maynard too. But in Bloomsbury it was more complicated: literally because 46 Gordon Square had been regarded as home by Vanessa and Clive Bell, who resented their eviction and banned Lydia from their Sussex retreat at Charleston (where the *Economic Consequences* had once been written).

Moreover 'Bloomsbury' in a figurative sense was likewise closed to Lydia, at least initially. It was not until the 1930s that she was admitted to the Memoir Club, part of a reconciliation eased by a deepening friendship between the Keyneses and the Woolfs. And since each of these couples now also had their own houses in Sussex, it could be said that Bloomsbury migrated. One key step was Maynard's acquisition of his farmhouse at Tilton in the 1920s, piquantly close to the Bells' house at Charleston, and only a few miles from the Woolfs' cottage at Rodmell. He was to write much of his *Treatise on Money* (1930) and his *General Theory* (1936) at Tilton, meanwhile spending the middle of the week at Gordon Square, usually with a long weekend during the university term in Cambridge, where he and Lydia were eventually to occupy a flat just off King's Parade. Not many dons led such a complicated and unconventional life, and with distinct but overlapping circles of friends.

As we have seen, Keynes's career cannot be comprehended by applying the template of the university structure or idiom of today. Despite his burgeoning fame, he did not seek appointment as a professor, at Cambridge or elsewhere. He was content to remain a Fellow of King's, where he was highly active, notably in serving as college Bursar from 1924 until his death, with responsibility for building the assets of an institution that he loved. Although he did not hold a formal appointment in the Faculty of Economics and Politics, he regularly gave lectures under its auspices; these took place in the University's spacious new Mill Lane lecture rooms from 1932 and had already become celebrity events, often packed to the doors.

As one student recalled, 'quite a number of people used to come up from London to attend his lectures, and the atmosphere was one of public performance rather than of academic discourse' (Rymes 1989, 17). Keynes made no pretence of offering a systematic course of instruction for the Tripos, such as a university lecturer would naturally feel obliged to provide; instead he was using this forum, among others, to put across his own current thinking. Some undergraduates found this frustrating and could only make sense of what he was saying in retrospect; or they simply stopped attending. Others were more receptive to the sense of theatre that was generated. 'It was as if we were listening to Charles Darwin or Isaac Newton', one American student recalled. 'The audience sat hushed as Keynes spoke' (Straight 1983, 57). This was the forum in which he chose to broach his current thinking at an early stage – both the *Treatise on Money* and the *General Theory* were initially presented to undergraduates and to fellow economists in this way.

Keynes's lifetime list of publications would serve as a rather odd curriculum vitae; and even those of his books with the most direct academic appeal would raise some eyebrows if submitted in a modern research assessment exercise. The *Treatise* indeed did the trick for him in securing academic recognition; but some of its most telling points are made with a characteristic brio that bursts bounds and confounds conventions. Thus the 'fundamental equations', laid out over four pages early in the first volume, duly convey the important distinction made between investment and saving; but 'a further elucidation' then follows up in a different idiom altogether. Consider the 'banana parable'.

'Let us suppose a community owning banana plantations and labouring to cultivate and collect bananas and nothing else; and consuming bananas and nothing else', we are enjoined. What this community does not spend on the consumption of bananas, it saves for new investment. So far, so good; but then comes the fall. 'Into this Eden there enters a thrift campaign, urging the members of the public to abate their improvident practices of devoting nearly all their current incomes to buying bananas for daily food'. What then? The same crop of bananas may be produced – but their price falls through the cuts necessarily made in people's purchasing power in order to finance their enhanced savings. 'This is splendid, or seems so', we read, since the cost of living has been reduced. But it is not really such a happy ending, as of course becomes apparent when the entrepreneurs suffer trade losses, and they naturally 'seek to protect themselves by throwing their employees out of work or reducing their wages'. Alas, this means an equivalent cut in the spending power of the public, in a vicious spiral where no equilibrium can be reached, with only three possible outcomes. Either all production of bananas ceases and the population starves; or the thrift campaign collapses; or investment is stimulated (JMK 5:158–60).

Of course, it would be an exaggeration to say that in three pages we have the kernel of the Keynesian revolution. Nonetheless we should never mistake the author's propensity to communicate his central insights through such literary devices rather than in more conventional didactic forms. We can likewise note how mathematicians as adept as himself and Frank Ramsey sometimes simply resorted to vernacular common sense. And we can also understand what Keynes warned students in his lectures, when seeking to convey his new theory of effective demand in 1933: 'These equations are merely a means of exposition and not a predictive tool. The real tool is thought, and they are not a substitute for it, but at most a guide or embodiment' (Clarke 1988, 258). Keynes was even to comment in the *General Theory*: 'Too large a proportion of recent "mathematical" economics are merely concoctions, as imprecise as the initial assumptions they rest on, which allow the author to lose sight of the complexities and interdependencies of the real world in a maze of pretentious and unhelpful symbols' (JMK 7:298). Thus spoke the former Twelfth Wrangler in the Mathematics Tripos of 1905.

Here is one reason why, among the economists at Cambridge, Keynes found a happy companion for many years in Dennis Robertson, whose own academic path had been initially via Part 1 of the Classics Tripos. When, as was common under the Cambridge Tripos system, Robertson had changed to the Economics Tripos in Part 2, he had subsequently been supervised by Keynes himself. A protégé who became a friend, Robertson trod his own path. His addiction to literary conceits made Lewis Carroll's *Alice* a favourite source; while this amused Keynes, it baffled many younger colleagues in the Economics Faculty.

Indeed, rather than having 'colleagues' in an institutional sense, it might be said that Keynes had friends: a highly select few of whom were important to him as fellow economists. Such a list would inevitably begin with the great Alfred Marshall. A long, respectful obituary notice on him was composed in 1924 during a blissful summer at Tilton, spent with Lydia – and indeed also with the recently bereaved Mary Paley Marshall, a strong early supporter of their relationship. 'The best thing Maynard ever did', she later told Harrod (Harrod 1951, 365). Maynard in turn was careful to show his appreciation of the widow's helpfulness in giving him unique access to the Marshall papers: a degree of license that he was careful not to compromise, even if it meant making some cuts in what he had written at the proof stage (Groenewegen 1995, 15–16,

748n). The resulting memoir of Marshall is one of Keynes's finest achievements in this genre, rightly commanding a place in his *Essays in Biography* (1933). Keynes wrote this as the editor of the *Economic Journal*, in which it first appeared; but it was also his tribute to a former family friend, with nothing in it that would have offended either Marshall's widow or his former henchman, John Neville Keynes, when he read it in Harvey Road. Yet in Maynard's own lectures, as student notes from 1933 confirm, he was sometimes freer and less reverential in his throwaway lines – 'This is characteristic of Marshall. You can't find much truth in him, and yet you cannot convict him of error' (Rymes 1989, 121).

By that time, Marshall's successor in his chair at Cambridge had, for the last twenty-five years, been A. C. Pigou. He was a Fellow of King's College, like Keynes himself; he too had served as President of the Cambridge Union Society. Always a loner, Pigou was politically advanced in his views, a pioneer of welfare economics, and in the First World War had been a conscientious objector (which accounts for the lateness of his election as a Fellow of the British Academy, belatedly achieved with Keynes's support in 1927, two years before he himself was elected). Pigou had come to economics via the Historical Tripos. In his lectures he became famous for telling his students 'it's all in Marshall'; and he followed Marshall in shunning professional controversy.

In this respect, Keynes did not reciprocate: at least not in his *General Theory* (1936), which singled out Pigou as a straw man for criticism. A footnote to the very first paragraph warns that the book's (now pejorative) term 'classical economists' would include those economists 'who adopted and perfected the theory of the Ricardian economics, including (for example) J.S. Mill, Marshall, Edgeworth and Prof. Pigou' (JMK 7:3n). Edgeworth, at Oxford, had remained Marshall's great disciple, so this indeed identified an apostolic succession – with Keynes now as the apostate. Thus the author should hardly have been surprised that his *General Theory* received a stinging academic review from Pigou, scorning his colleague's arrogant pose as the Einstein of economic theory. Yet Keynes reacted by telling Robertson: 'I was distressed by the Prof's review and even more so that you should think it worthy of him' (JMK 14:87). It was more like an affront to a code of friendship than a professional academic disagreement; but it blew over, with Pigou and Keynes, both Fellows of King's, continuing to dine together at high table.

***

Keynes's incipient breach with Robertson himself was a different matter: more personal, more painful and more protracted. As we have seen, Robertson's influence in developing the distinction between the concepts of saving and investment had been fundamental in shaping the analysis of the *Treatise on Money* in the late 1920s. Little wonder that, after this work was published in 1930, Keynes wished to continue their partnership by now submitting to Robertson the successive drafts of a projected new work. Yet by the summer of 1933, it was clear that this new book did not make happy reading for Robertson, with its increasing evidence of Keynes's readiness to stir up just the sort of controversy between economists that Robertson found so upsetting. 'What a ghastly subject it is!' he expostulated to Keynes. 'Here are you saying wage reductions are no good, and Pigou saying they are a lot of good. ... How I wish we could form a Cambridge front again!' (JMK 13:313–14).

It was too late. Keynes's mind was now set on its course, once he came to perceive that the real problem might not centre on the role of interest rate in equilibrating the economy through matching saving and investment – which had been essentially a theoretical elaboration of how the gold standard *ought* to work. But now the early proofs of Keynes's new book, loyally but sadly perused by Robertson, pointed increasingly in other directions. And these proofs were also read, though with more sustained sympathy, by Ralph Hawtrey, long established as the Treasury's pre-eminent adviser on theoretical issues.

Hawtrey's connection with Keynes went back to their days together as Apostles at Cambridge; and they had happily served together in the wartime Treasury. Although it was an academic article published by Hawtrey in 1925 that provided the intellectual authority for the 'Treasury View', as famously affirmed by Churchill in 1929, Hawtrey had entered one crucial caveat in supporting the official line. In his analysis, expansion of credit was the real answer to unemployment – public works 'merely a piece of ritual' – and in this expansionist stance he tacitly agreed with much of what the *Treatise* argued. Hawtrey was not only 'most nearly on the right track' in Keynes's eyes, but was indeed ready to declare to the Macmillan Committee that 'the way to conjure outlay out of the fourth dimension is to lower Bank Rate' (Clarke 1988, 52, 143, 146). Hence Keynes's comment to him: 'although we always seem to differ on these monetary questions in discussion, I feel that ultimately I am joined in common agreement with you as against most of the rest of the world' (JMK 13:132).

What had troubled Hawtrey was the *Treatise*'s insistence (which was sustained by Robertson, of course) on defining saving and investment so that they might differ. Accordingly, what Hawtrey saw as a crucial point was that any increase in investment would consequently increase the income of consumers, who would pass on part of it through their spending. Here, we might think, was a pioneering suggestion of a process rather like that which Keynes's young collaborator, Richard Kahn, was shortly to identify – subsequently famous as 'the multiplier'. But two points need to be borne in mind. One is that Kahn's concept only acquired this name and fame when appropriated and publicised by Keynes in 1933; and the other is that, when Hawtrey himself had had the opportunity of publishing his own novel and arresting thoughts, it was (perversely) this very part of his exposition that he chose to omit! (Deutscher 1990, 103–5).

Hawtrey thus concealed, for the next half a century, his own potential claims to originality here. Here was a further difference in temperament from Keynes, whom he continued to advise: wisely and discreetly (as befitted a man who was to become a 'Treasury knight' a few years later) and with the mutual tolerance of old friends. Keynes gratefully accepted some of Hawtrey's criticisms. 'You have taken amazing pains about my book', he wrote in June 1932. 'I only wish others had taken as much trouble'. But he also gave Hawtrey due warning: 'I am working it out all over again'. This time Keynes would acknowledge that saving and investment indeed had to be defined as equal, with increments of expenditure bringing this about, and it was thus 'much preferable to use a term about which everyone agrees' (JMK 13:172). Only later, once the publication of the *General Theory* had failed to persuade Hawtrey, did Keynes become reluctantly convinced 'that nothing that I can say will open your eyes – I do not say to the truth of my argument – but to what the essence of my argument, true or false, actually is' (JMK 14:23).

Keynes had a different problem in excusing to Robertson his apparent betrayal of their common insistence that saving and investment could differ. Keynes tried putting it in this way in early 1932: 'The old "common-sense" view not only held that savings and investment are necessarily equal (as – we have seen – *in a sense* they are), but inferred from this that therefore one need not bother' (JMK 13:278). The real problem was thus the process by which this outcome was achieved. The amount that would *actually* be saved, rather than the speculative amount that had originally been hoped, was what counted. And such an outcome was by no means the 'the voluntary result of virtuous decisions' and therefore 'no longer the dog, which common sense believes it to be, but the tail' (JMK 13:276). Thus it was now the Keynesian dog called investment that wagged its tail called savings.

This was how Keynes explained himself to his old friends, Hawtrey and Robertson; but the drafts of his new book had three other readers of a younger generation who were to be thanked in the preface of the *General Theory*. There was Roy Harrod, born 1900, then a lecturer in economics at Oxford and later Keynes's loyal biographer. Two further names were closely allied. One was that of Richard Kahn, born 1905; as a Fellow of King's, he naturally saw much of

Keynes, whose indispensable aide he became. Keynes also thanked Joan Robinson, born 1903, an assistant lecturer in the Economics Faculty at Cambridge – a dynamic, left-wing influence, much reviled by Robertson, but close to Kahn. Indeed she had begun an affair with him, and in early 1932 Maynard reported wryly to Lydia that he had disturbed them together on the floor of his study in King's – no doubt, he surmised, 'the conversation was only on The Pure Theory of Monopoly' (Skidelsky 1992, 448–9). All this could be said between friends, uncensoriously, with many allowances made accordingly.

The publication of Kahn's seminal article in the *Economic Journal* in 1931, introducing what became the multiplier, was an outcome of his participation in an informal seminar with four other economists of a younger generation in Cambridge, dubbed 'the circus'. Their thinking had indeed prompted Keynes towards the formulation of his new theory in the academic year 1930–1. For Kahn's argument helped to justify public investment as a remedy for unemployment by showing its knock-on effects through the increased consumer spending of those put into work. Moreover, this article crucially incorporated a generalisation, contributed by James Meade, born 1907; he was visiting from Oxford for a year, during which he too had become a member of the circus. This addition to the article was 'Mr Meade's Relation', as Kahn termed it in acknowledgement that it was 'far more important' in its implications than his own estimate of the employment multiplier. For what it demonstrated was how, as well as the impact of public works in boosting spending, increments of saving were reciprocally generated – thus identifying the available resources that paid for the initial investment (Kahn 1984, 98–9). All of this fed into the analytical synthesis that was to become the *General Theory*.

Joan Robinson subsequently never let anyone forget her own tutelary role as a member of the circus. Her view was that 'there were moments when we had some trouble in getting Maynard to see what the point of his revolution really was, but when he came to sum it up after the book was published he got it into focus' (Keynes 1975, 125). A further member of the circus was her husband Austin Robinson, born 1897, a lecturer in the Economics Faculty and soon a key assistant for Keynes in editing the *Economic Journal*. Robinson's own considered view was that Keynes 'had a wonderful memory for arguments, but no memory for their authors' (Robinson 1947, 67). About such intellectual pilfering, Robinson bore no grudges; he was nothing if not a tolerant man.

The fifth member of the circus was Piero Sraffa, born in 1898: a reclusive Italian scholar with a long-standing academic foothold in Cambridge, whose diligent research on the history of economic thought left its mark on the exposition of what became the *General Theory*. For that book begins with its declaration of war on the 'classical economics' of the followers of Ricardo, an economist on whom Sraffa was to become the great authority. Keynes's own essay on Ricardo's rival, Malthus, proclaiming him the real father of a concept of 'effective demand', was finished in 1932, duly declaring its author's debt to Sraffa, 'from whom nothing is hid' (JMK 10:97).

Prompted by the circus, Keynes thus came to identify effective demand as the root of the problem. Driven by investment, total income would increase. And investment and savings were thus indeed always equal, whatever the level of 'Bank rate'. In which case, understanding the role of the rate of interest was another kind of problem with another kind of answer – in fact, determined by a variable *demand for money itself*. And here it was the state of confidence that mattered, influencing people either optimistically to tie up their money in investments, or pessimistically to hold their savings in cash. Thus the prevailing interest rate was the measure of what Keynes now identified as 'liquidity preference'. As he put it later to his biographer Harrod, such a link 'became quite clear in my mind the moment I thought of it' (JMK 14:84–5). And this moment had certainly come by the time Keynes gave his fourth university lecture on 31 October 1932, with his declaration that 'in itself the rate of interest is an *expression of liquidity preference*', as duly recorded, with due emphasis, by an attentive student in Mill Lane (Rymes 1989, 69).

The new analysis informed the pamphlet that Keynes published in 1933, on both sides of the Atlantic, as 'The Means to Prosperity': policy advice that was, in a sense, a trailer for the *General Theory* (1936). The book itself, flaunting its iconoclastic pretensions to novelty as against 'classical economics', inevitably disconcerted Robertson, for reasons as much temperamental as intellectual in origin. 'You are like a man searching for a formula by which he can agree without changing his mind. So unlike me!' Keynes wrote to him at the end of 1936, now insisting: 'The last thing I should accuse you of is being classical or orthodox. But you won't slough your skins like a good snake!' (JMK 14:94–5). The rupture in their relationship never really healed. Though both men regretted it, the fact that Robertson was not acknowledged in the preface of the *General Theory* spoke for itself; references to him in the text were stilted – maybe the truth, but hardly the whole truth. Subsequent factionalism in the Cambridge Economics Faculty saw Joan Robinson emerging as the standard-bearer for an interpretation of Keynesianism in which she had a vested interest. And here was a conflict that left Keynes uneasy. 'The trouble between Joan and Dennis (which I thought I had settled) may crop up again', Maynard reported to Lydia in March 1936. 'He's getting dangerously near to trying to prevent her from lecturing; and if he were to succeed, the state of rift between the older people and the younger would be dreadful' (Moggridge 1992, 600). Keynes's ethos allowed for friends to disagree, even in ways that became quite pointed, but did not license ideological vendettas of the kind now emerging in the 1930s.

Marshall would indeed have been horrified. Looking back after Keynes's death in 1946, Pigou showed great magnanimity in his own comments. 'Keynes's life was cast in times more troubled than Marshall's, times of violent upheaval and rapid world-wide dislocations', he wrote in his obituary notice for the British Academy. Keynes had accordingly adopted 'a less leisured approach' than Marshall. 'In my personal opinion, between this approach and Marshall's there is no essential conflict', Pigou maintained; but he also added a tribute of touching humility: 'Not a little of what we now believe ourselves to have known all along it may well be that we really owe to him' (Pigou 1946, 407, 411).

8

Truths between Friends
Bloomsbury and Politics

As we have seen in previous chapters, Keynes was concerned with political problems in a far more persistent and fundamental way than has often been credited. His important career steps as a protégé of Edwin Montagu had owed much to their mutual commitment to Liberal party politics; both had served as undergraduates in the taxing role of President of the Cambridge Union Society, always a highly politicised institution; Keynes had continued to participate in its debates in the years before the First World War as well as serving in Liberal and Free Trade organisations. 'Keynes's absorbing interest at this stage of his life was politics', as Austin Robinson well appreciated (Robinson 1947, 10).

Keynes's own relations with 'the Great Ones' had brought his successive connections with Asquith and with Lloyd George into an obvious conflict, which we have seen him seeking to resolve in different ways. Thus the young Treasury-minded recruit was initially pitted against Lloyd George's 'proto-Keynesian' hunches on Britain's potential capacity to wage war; it was Keynes who had assumed a 'classical' position on the economy's inelasticity, focusing on displacement effects within a fixed aggregate limit. Of course, this is to take a rather theoretical view of such differences in economic analysis – which is hardly how Lloyd George would have expressed his hunches at the time. Keynes too was a political animal in a more direct and obvious dimension. He continued to admire Asquith's record as Prime Minister of a great reforming government, with monuments like old age pensions and national insurance for health and unemployment. Hence the tribute to Asquith in Keynes's 1928 obituary essay: 'It is remarkable, looking back on the Liberal legislation of the eight years before the war, to see how abundant it was, yet how well chosen, and how completely on the whole it has stood the test of events' (JMK 10:39).

Conversely, his retrospective view of Lloyd George (in 1939) was unforgiving: 'of the two dark deeds of his career, the Treaty of Versailles and the slaughter of organised liberalism, we are suffering as much today from the second as from the first' (JMK 21:494). What Asquithians always recalled in retailing such grudges was that Lloyd George had used the famous 'Maurice debate' in the House of Commons in May 1918 to divide the Liberal Party. And the ostensible issue here was whether, as Prime Minister, Lloyd George had misled the House about the number of British troops available for combat in the desperate final struggle in northern France – an allegation publicly made (at the expense of his own military career) by Major-General Sir Frederick Maurice. Considered as an exercise in 'ruthless truth-telling', Maurice could be said to have anticipated the *Economic Consequences* by more than a year. The facts in this complex matter continued to be disputed long after Keynes's own death, with dedicated historians spending whole chapters in elucidation of the conflicting evidence that eventually emerged, piece by piece. Of such details Keynes was necessarily unaware; but what he knew was that the noble Asquithian hero Maurice was the father of Joan Robinson. It was a small world.

Keynes had, of course, gone on to make himself Lloyd George's arch-critic over the Versailles Treaty (though obscuring for posterity his own role over its searing provision on War Guilt). Yet reconciliation with the Celtic 'syren' had subsequently seen them cooperating closely in bringing the issue of unemployment to the fore in the 1920s. In the 1929 general election campaign Keynes had been as prominent in debate as any Liberal except Lloyd George himself. The 'Treasury View' was now their target, with Keynes's arguments deployed against his old colleagues. It was the economic cataclysm of 1931, sweeping away the minority Labour government and the gold standard alike, that signalled a final rupture here. 'You ought to keep in touch with Maynard Keynes in a crisis like this', Lloyd George was advised, only to respond: 'I have been in touch with that hedgehog before now' (Jones 1954, 19).

In the 1930s the Liberal Party split into three factions. Of these, one got itself swallowed up by the so-called National Government, another remained loftily but impotently apart, the third consisted mainly of Lloyd George's own family. Keynes was stranded, most of his younger associates now supporting the Labour Party: Joan Robinson, Richard Kahn, James Meade and Roy Harrod all active in the New Fabian Research Bureau. Likewise the political orientation of the late Frank Ramsey's close friend Kingsley Martin: a socialist and an aspiring academic who had failed to get elected, despite Keynes's ostensible support, to a Fellowship at King's, and subsequently made a highly successful career in journalism. It was Martin whom Keynes supported as the new editor when his own Liberal weekly paper, the *Nation*, amalgamated with the socialist weekly, the *New Statesman*, in 1931. Keynes, who had previously chaired the board of the *Nation*, now chaired the new joint editorial board. The fact that the *New Statesman* normally supported the Labour Party was not in itself a problem; but the young editor naturally took account of the views on policy urged, sometimes in very forthright terms, by the chairman of the board. The two of them often met for lunch, or for dinner at the Keynes residence in Gordon Square, though Maynard would make clear that seeing Lydia was his priority if he had just returned from his weekly stint in Cambridge. Part of Keynes's London life, Martin was not often invited to Tilton (unlike Richard Kahn who would work there with Keynes on successive drafts of the *General Theory*, currently being written during the Cambridge vacations).

There was a copious Keynes–Martin editorial correspondence which also generated some contributions for publication in the *New Statesman* – over two hundred pages in all in Volume 28 of the *Collected Writings*. The letters that Keynes sent were candid and forthright, and he sometimes had to apologise if one that he had failed to mark 'personal' had been opened by the staff at the *New Statesman*. One thing that stands out is the degree of political engagement that Keynes continued to display, not just on economic issues, as in the 1920s, but from 1933 at least, on foreign policy too.

The two fields were obviously linked, not least in this period because many British socialists were inclined to take a favourable view of the great experiment under way in Stalin's Russia; Martin often did so. The venerable prophets of the Fabian Society, founded in the late nineteenth century to proclaim the inevitability of gradualism, remained prominent figures in the 1930s. Sidney and Beatrice Webb were to visit Russia and write a huge book, more often cited than read, about Soviet Communism, proclaiming it 'a new civilisation'. Prior to that, Bernard Shaw and H. G. Wells had clashed prominently in the pages of the *New Statesman* in 1934 over the significance of the Russian experiment. Keynes joined in, affecting to 'pay my affectionate respects to both our grand old schoolmasters, Shaw and Wells, to whom most of us have gone to school all our lives, our divinity master and our stinks master' (JMK 28:25).

Keynes had already made his own position clear. 'Marxists are ready to sacrifice the political liberties of individuals in order to change the existing economic order. So are Fascists and Nazis', he had written in a letter to the editor in August 1934, then affirming: 'My own aim is economic reform by the methods of political liberalism' (JMK 28:28–9). Keynes elaborated on this stance in his ensuing controversy with Shaw that autumn, offering two linked propositions. 'The standard system is based on intellectual error', he asserted, arguing not only that economic orthodoxy was inherently flawed in its doctrine but also that it was now outmoded: 'The facts of the world shift' (JMK 28:32). Hence Keynes's opportunity, now implicitly claiming if not yet explicitly stating that the forthcoming publication of the *General Theory* would clinch his argument, in an era when a 'Salariat' rather than a Proletariat now called the shots. 'The problem to-day is first to concert good advice and then to convince the well-intentioned that it is good' (JMK 28:34).

It was Dora Russell (wife of Bertrand, an old Cambridge friend of Keynes) who then posed the reasonable question, that if it was all quite so easy, why had Keynes not prevailed thus far? 'Because I have not yet succeeded in convincing either the expert or the ordinary man that I am right. If I am wrong, this will prove to have been fortunate', he responded. 'If, however, I am right, it is, I feel certain, only a matter of time before I convince both; and when both are convinced, economic policy will, with the usual time lag, follow suit'. This wild claim could be read as echoing his published views on inside and outside opinion; or as anticipating the final paragraph of the *General Theory*, about the relative potency of ideas as against vested interests. Here it was framed in specifically British terms, reflecting his working assumptions at the time. 'In this country henceforward power will normally reside with the Left. The Labour Party will always have a majority, except when something has happened to raise a doubt in the minds of reasonable and disinterested persons whether the Labour Party are in the right' (JMK 28:35–6).

This political declaration was published in the *New Statesman* for 24 November 1934. It was only a few weeks later, at the beginning of January 1935, that Maynard and Lydia Keynes were visited at Tilton by two members of the Labour Party: their close friends Leonard and Virginia Woolf, who now had their own Sussex cottage a few miles away at Rodmell. It was more comfortable at Tilton, with six on the staff, than at Rodmell, where 'the Woolves' now purported to manage without servants, though often invisibly supported by domestic 'help'. After lunch had been cooked for them all, Maynard read out to his guests, first, the long letter that he had meanwhile received from Shaw, recapitulating his assertions about Marx; and then read his own reply.

As Virginia's diary put it:

> [H]e thinks he has revolutionized economics; in the new book he is writing. 'Wait ten years, & let it absorb the politics & the psychology & so on that will accrue to it; & then you'll see – the old Ricardo system will be exposed; & the whole thing set on a new footing'. This he wrote in so many words: a gigantic boast; true I daresay. (VWD 4:272).

Virginia's apt summary catches the tone and import; she was not only well used to Maynard's gigantic boasts but had learned to take some of them seriously, certainly on economic matters, albeit less trustingly on politics and foreign affairs.

***

In his writings in the *New Statesman* Keynes repeatedly urged the need for Britain and France (and also sometimes Russia) to take the lead against what he usually termed 'the brigand powers', meaning Germany and Italy (and sometimes Japan). But he was well aware of the difficulties, not least because of the inconsistencies of British left-wingers, often torn between piously professing support for the League of Nations but – when it came to the crunch over the Italian invasion of Abyssinia in 1935 – opting out of any consequential action. And the outbreak of the Spanish civil war a year later sharpened the dilemma.

It was easy enough to dismiss actually aiding the brigand powers. But whether to intervene against them or to stand aloof was a choice on which (in a letter in the *New Statesman* in August 1936) Keynes confessed that 'I do not myself know my own mind' – moreover advising that 'I doubt if it is wise, as yet, to reach a firm conclusion'. This sounded distinctly more pragmatic than principled. Keynes's published letter further suggested, in a tart comment on Martin's most recent leading article, that Baldwin, currently the Conservative Prime Minister, 'is perhaps wiser than you are. He may be hesitating because he knows that nothing is certain. ... Something totally unexpected may suddenly change the whole situation' (JMK 28:49). It is an interesting train of thought and worth exploring further, not only in this immediate context, but as an indication of the way that Keynes's own mind was moving on issues of probability that we know had long concerned him.

Perhaps in politics the unexpected often happens; conversely the expectations aroused by politicians might prove self-confirming. Certainly Keynes was already on record in urging the Chancellor of the Exchequer in the National Government (Neville Chamberlain) to relax his self-defeating norms of austerity by taking a more optimistic view of the facts before him. 'If he does, he will help to bring the facts in sight, which would justify the optimism that he has adopted' (JMK 21:153). Keynes had spoken in such terms in a radio broadcast in January 1933; and he was to repeat his advice in print a few months later: 'Unfortunately, the more pessimistic the Chancellor's policy, the more likely it is that the pessimistic anticipations will be realized and vice versa. Whatever the Chancellor dreams, will come true!' (JMK 21:184). This was

179

in April 1933, a month after President Roosevelt's inaugural address with its famous claim 'that the only thing we have to fear is fear itself'. Little wonder that Keynes looked westward, where the land was bright, for practical inspiration.

Chapter 12 of the *General Theory* was to be called 'The State of Long-term Expectation'. For in the performance of the economy, a crucial condition was the state of confidence at any one time; and its extreme precariousness was theoretically intractable. Hence the tacit agreement to fall back upon convention, and likewise the opportunities open to shrewd investors with strong nerves (maybe like Keynes himself in the currency market). 'The actual, private object of the most skilled investment to-day is "to beat the gun", as the Americans so well express it', he suggested; or it was like guessing the outcome of a beauty contest through a shrewd anticipation of how others would vote (JMK 7:149–58). Under such conditions the potent factor was 'animal spirits'. This was not presented as a new insight. It was a reminder 'that human decisions affecting the future, whether personal or political or economic, cannot depend on strict mathematical expectations, since the basis for making such calculations does not exist', Keynes argued, in terms as blunt as Ramsey had often used (JMK 7:162–3).

With his newly published *General Theory* stimulating international discussion of what it really meant, Keynes offered some hints to clarify his position. Privately, in May 1936, he wrote to his old colleague (and disillusioned former collaborator) Hubert Henderson, musing about 'a world ruled by uncertainty with an uncertain future linked to an actual present', and its economic implications

(JMK 14:222). This sounded very much like the world he described Baldwin as confronting a few months later. And in the autumn of that year, when Keynes gave a lecture in Stockholm about his new theory, his surviving notes (JMK 14:100) show him dwelling on a further problem in making himself understood:

> What I have to say intrinsically easy
> Difficulty lies in its running against our habitual modes of thought
> It is only to an audience of economists that it is difficult.

Keynes, anxious to make himself clear, was now composing a scholarly article that was rushed into print in the (American) *Quarterly Journal of Economics*. For his academic readers, he offered what has often been read as his final testament on his own methodology. 'Perhaps the reader feels that this general, philosophical disquisition on the behavior of mankind is somewhat remote from the economic theory under discussion', he acknowledged (JMK 14:115). For what he introduced was an explicit series of reflections on what he meant, not just by probability but by matters that were 'uncertain' in a more intractable way.

To the modern eye, Keynes's discussion seems to hark back to issues with which he had indeed found himself entangled when he had published his own *Treatise on Probability* – and on which, in the same year, the Chicago economist Frank Knight had published his study *Risk, Uncertainty and Profit* (1921). Yet these were two ships that passed in the fog; neither seems to have benefited from a sympathetic reading of the works of the other, as historians have long recognised

(Bateman 1996, 129). Chicago was a long way from Cambridge; neither side showed much inclination to engage.

Uncertainty itself was the issue here. 'The sense in which I am using the term', Keynes wrote in 1937, 'is that in which the prospect of a European war is uncertain, or the price of copper and the rate of interest twenty years hence, or the obsolescence of a new invention, or the position of private wealth owners in the social system in 1970' (JMK 14:113–14). Today we may claim to know the correct answers on all these matters. We are thus now better informed than Keynes had been – but not necessarily 'wiser', in the sense that he had judged Baldwin 'wiser' in 1936 for recognising that 'nothing is certain' when contemplating the prospect of a European war.

In Keynes's view, it was a time to reserve judgement and for the left to refrain from posturing, especially given that its tender-minded constituency was torn between vocally supporting the League while actually denying it any means of effective action. He made such points knowing that this might hurt many of his close friends. Keynes's own rueful conclusion was clear: he declared that 'the argument that it is dangerous to-day that only the brigand powers should possess armaments carries conviction' (JMK 28:53). He saw no immediate route of escape from this quandary: 'The fatal dilemma arises precisely because the Fascist Powers are readier to go to war for their objects than we are for ours' (JMK 28:55). In a world in which calculations of probabilities had to yield to imperatives hedged about by uncertainty, hard choices needed to be faced. 'It is our duty to prolong peace, hour by hour, day by day, for as long as we can', he wrote in July 1937. 'We do not know what the future will bring, except that it will be quite different from anything we could predict' (JMK 28:62).

***

'Truth and wit are felt by many to be rather shocking virtues which should appear in public only if they are decently veiled' (JMK 10:388). These are the words of Keynes's old Bloomsbury friend David Garnett in his introduction to *Two Memoirs*, published in 1949, three years after Keynes's death. It comprised not only the text of 'Dr Melchior' but also one other paper that Keynes had given to the Memoir Club. This was 'My Early Beliefs', given in September 1938. The fact that the paper has been quoted so copiously in modern writings on Keynes and Bloomsbury has perhaps provided its own justification for letting it 'appear in public', notwithstanding Garnett's obvious apprehensions in following the directions in Keynes's will. But that leaves open a question over the memoir's literal truth, for all its literary wit.

'I went up to Cambridge at Michaelmas 1902, and Moore's Principia Ethica came out at the end of my first year', Keynes had written. 'I have never heard of the present generation having read it'. This sly remark plainly referred to the contemporaries of the late Frank Ramsey, blatantly unimpressed by their elders' cult of 'Moorism'. Here was a lost world, ironically observed in retrospect, where the influence of Moore allegedly gave the young Apostles a 'religion' in trusting their own intuitions and states of mind, but left them unmoved by 'morals' about their obligations to follow social rules and conventions. 'To the consequences of having a religion and no morals I return later', Keynes declared (JMK 10:435–6). Leonard Woolf, with his abiding attachment to Moore's doctrines, lived long enough to see 'My Early Beliefs' taken literally; and he distanced himself from what he termed 'a fascinating, an extremely amusing account', for reasons that will become apparent (Woolf 1960, 144).

What is not in doubt is that the Apostolic connection was a real bond, not identical with that of 'Bloomsbury' nor the Memoir Club, but for Keynes integrally linked. When he found the Apostles in danger of institutional extinction after the First World War, he had sought to revive the society, not least by recruiting some senior members who had never been elected as undergraduates, like Dennis Robertson. Ralph Hawtrey was already an Apostle; both he and Robertson had been at Eton and Trinity. It was the journalist Desmond MacCarthy (also Eton and Trinity, and himself an Apostle) who had been instrumental, along with his wife Molly, in founding the Memoir Club in 1920. When she wrote to Keynes proposing the club she did not mention the name of Saxon Sydney-Turner; but he had been an Apostle, and a pre-war member of 'Old Blomsbury', introduced as such to Maynard's brother Geoffrey, who later commented: 'Saxon Sydney-Turner I had no way of knowing as he never opened his mouth, and I sometimes wondered why he was there at all' (Keynes 1981, 115). Inevitably, it seemed, the silent and unfathomable Sydney-Turner was to be included in Bloomsbury, and then in the Memoir Club, alongside his contemporaries at Trinity, Woolf and Strachey. These were all close friends who knew Keynes well through one or other of these frankly elitist connections.

It is worth pausing to reflect on the nature of this continuous thread, running through all the vicissitudes of Keynes's career: on how natural it all seemed to himself. Thus in a later phase, when Lord Keynes of Tilton went to Bretton Woods in July 1944, representing Churchill's government at a vitally important international conference, we have the testimony of a member of the British delegation, Lionel Robbins. He is remembered as not only a distinguished economist but also a felicitous diarist, who, on the opening day of the conference, found himself participating 'in a particularly *recherché* celebration'. It commemorated the 500th anniversary of 'the Concordat between King's College, Cambridge, and New College, Oxford' – with Keynes representing the former, Robbins the latter (as a former Fellow); Dennis Robertson invited to represent Eton; and two distinguished American officials (Dean Acheson and Oscar Cox) who represented Yale University as a sister foundation – which also happily qualified the leader of the Chinese delegation (Hsiang-His Kung). 'Keynes, who had been looking forward to the event for weeks as excitedly as a schoolboy, was at his most charming', Robbins recorded, with admiration but also with some bafflement: 'So radical in outlook in matters purely intellectual, in matters of culture he is a true Burkean conservative' (Robbins 1990, 167). None of this would have come as any surprise to Virginia Woolf, who was piquantly aware, not just of Maynard's own foibles, but of her friends' status, as men and as 'insiders'.

Of course, nobody talked of 'networking' in those days; they had only to look around them, not least when the Memoir Club met. What the club was offered by Keynes in his 1938 paper was tailored to an audience that he knew well and which, in turn knew well enough not to take him literally. What he suggested were tortuous definitions of the terms 'religion' and 'morals', open to challenge if only because Keynes's own conception of probability had offered a basis for actions to be judged on the basis of their likely consequences. In general, he had always acknowledged the social utility of rules and conventions ('morals'); but had argued that it might be justifiable for an individual to break them, and in this restricted sense become an 'immoralist', if this was likely to produce a better outcome. The tension between rules and discretion is surely a lurking but unvoiced issue here. Such had been Keynes's own justification in 1916 for resisting conscription for military service on principle, while reserving his own right to choose whether to volunteer (with the further twist that such a choice had not actually been necessary for a person employed on vital wartime Treasury work). So the key point was that *probable* consequences had to serve as a good enough guide. This is a sophisticated position, with long-term implications for Keynes's thinking.

Yet in 'My Early Beliefs' Keynes caricatures such views in a way that has predictably led many subsequent readers astray. 'We repudiated entirely customary morals, conventions and traditional wisdom. We were, that is to say, in the strict sense of the term, immoralists' (JMK 10:446). (Beguiling nonsense, thought Leonard Woolf.) Keynes's assertion is followed by another, equally sweeping: 'In short, we repudiated all versions of the doctrine of original sin, of there being insane and irrational springs of wickedness in most men'. And a natural consequence was that 'we completely misunderstood human nature, including our own' (JMK 10:447–8). The picture of this fools' paradise is built up successively towards inevitable climactic disillusion. Little wonder that such passages were to be seized upon by Keynes's critics from the moment the memoir was published in 1949 and over the succeeding decades. Here, it seems, is a damning indictment from his own pen: narcissistic, arrogant, feckless, irresponsible and, above all, naïve. Why Keynes wrote in quite this way in 1938 is perhaps worth exploring through other evidence.

***

Virginia Woolf's diary is a source that does not score very high on conventional economics citation indexes. Yet the fact that she and Keynes were the two figures of real genius in Bloomsbury did not escape either of these highly perceptive, highly intuitive, highly gifted writers. On being shown Keynes's *Tract on Monetary Reform* in 1923, she had written: 'as I truly said when he gave me some pages of his new book to read, the process of mind there displayed is as far ahead of me as Shakespeare's. True, I don't respect it so much' (VWD 2:266).

Virginia had taken time to get used to the marriage of Maynard and Lydia, though her initial scepticism gave way to a growing personal warmth. 'Dined with Lydia and Maynard: two couples, elderly, childless, distinguished', she had reported in 1928, when none of them was yet fifty.

> He and she both urbane and admirable. Grey comes at
> Maynard's temples. He is finer looking now: not with
> us pompous or great: simple, with his mind working
> always, on Russian Bolshevists, glands, genealogies;

always the proof of a remarkable mind when it overflows thus vigorously into byepaths ... Lydia is composed, and controlled. She says very sensible things. (VWD 3:181)

In the 1930s the Woolves and the Keyneses met regularly – not perhaps as often as they would have wished, but routinely around Christmas, as Virginia's diary records. In every year except one during the last decade of her life, she notes a Christmas reunion with the Keyneses, often for lunch or dinner on Christmas Day: the last one on Christmas Eve 1940, only a few months before her own death by drowning. 'The two of them were our dearest friends', Maynard was to tell his mother in relaying this shocking news (Skidelsky 2000, 87). This friendship had been maintained upon the Bloomsbury principles of deliberate candour tempered by personal affection.

In May 1938, Woolf had published her tract *Three Guineas*. It has a highly artificial structure, presented as an educated woman's response to three pleas for funds from societies aimed at preventing war. These structural problems in exposition undoubtedly make it hard work to get to the motherlode and only in the late twentieth century did *Three Guineas* attain the status of a classic feminist text. Though it had created quite a splash on publication, Leonard Woolf was not alone in thinking it her worst book. The theme, that a male-dominated structure of education had bred militarism, was feelingly developed. Virginia's own sense of grievance was not only well-rehearsed but surely well-merited. She had indeed been denied the sort of education at Cambridge that was inevitably offered to her brothers, Adrian and Thoby. When she wrote in *Three Guineas* of the peremptory demands of 'Arthur's education fund' on an upper-middle-class family budget, an implicit target is obviously the failings of Leslie Stephen himself to give his talented daughter the opportunities she had deserved. She observed that 'the noble courts and quadrangles of Oxford and Cambridge often appear to educated men's daughters like petticoats with holes in them, cold legs of mutton, and the boat train starting for abroad while the guard slams the door in their faces' (Woolf 1938, 8).

Hence the emotional charge that animated Woolf's proposal of an Outsiders Society: 'It would consist of educated men's daughters working in their own class – how indeed can they work in any other? – and by their own methods for liberty, equality and peace' (Woolf 1938, 122). As an outsider, then, she would not ask a brother to fight for 'our' country – the response should instead be to say: 'in fact as a woman, I have no country. As a woman I want no country' (Woolf 1938, 125). Her tract was published in August 1938, only months after the Nazis had taken over Austria and with the fate of Czechoslovakia now hanging in the balance. It was a moment of truth for the British liberal left, including Leonard Woolf and Maynard Keynes, of course. Various strategies were canvassed: to get the Labour Party to support rearmament, to support a popular front against fascism, even to consider cooperation with the reactionary imperialist Churchill.

The question of the hour was: how on earth to stop Hitler except by military force? 'The small boy struts and trumpets outside the window: implore him to stop; he goes on; say nothing he stops'. This was the response suggested in *Three Guineas*: that a duty 'to maintain an attitude of complete indifference' is the method available to daughters of educated men 'to prevent war and to ensure freedom' (Woolf 1938, 126). In context, it was perhaps not simply misogynistic to find this unconvincing or even frivolous as a response to the immediate threat of Nazi domination.

'Maynard sends for us on Wednesday; is said by Lydia to be very critical of 3 Gs', Virginia noted in her diary at Rodmell on 22 August 1938. She had to steel herself for the encounter at Tilton, as she admitted the next day: 'It is odd to be as nervous as I am at the idea of seeing Maynard tomorrow, and his heckling: dear old Hitler' (VWD 5:163). The mocking gibes that she anticipated, however, were not delivered, as she later noted with some relief. 'By the way Maynard never said a word. Some were unsaid. As for instance, Lydia: we all put up with you Virginia, said significantly, kissing me at parting. M. tired, extended, rather grim. But emotion had to be restrained' (VWD 5:163–4).

It should be remembered, in these exchanges, that Maynard was now a sick man, needing to husband his energies after the onset in 1937 of his serious heart problems, with Lydia's support more indispensable than ever. But he had persisted in his full range of activities; he continued to propagate his economic analysis in disseminating the *General Theory*; he remained editor of the *Economic Journal*; he also retained his chairman's role at the *New Statesman*; and he continued to enjoy the companionship of his old friends, more often now in Sussex than in Bloomsbury itself.

Keynes gave his own paper 'My Early Beliefs' to the Memoir Club at Tilton at 5 p.m. on Sunday 11 September 1938. He had written it in the previous couple of weeks, still an invalid, currently much agitated about the impending fate of Czechoslovakia, corresponding almost daily with Kingsley Martin about the crisis. Indeed Martin had evidently been fended off by Lydia when he had tried to telephone earlier in the day – 'I had finished a long bit of dictating only a minute before you rang up', Maynard explained to him (JMK 28:120). His message for the editor was to avoid mention of adjusting the border in the Sudetenland, even though such revision along ethnic lines had much to be said for it in principle. Indeed both Keynes and Martin were agreed on this objective; but the *New Statesman*'s error had been to broach such a possibility prematurely. Hence Keynes's immediate point: 'I was simply trying to be emphatic about what you say yourself – that it is plain as a pikestaff that at this juncture one must back up the Czechs, and particularly *not* suggest to Hitler that he can get what to him seems more' (JMK 28:119). If it was a bluff, it was a necessary one in a tense standoff to face down Hitler, strutting and trumpeting outside the window.

Here, then, was the immediate context for 'My Early Beliefs', the ink on it barely dry, the crisis at the back of the minds of the dozen close friends in the room, but Maynard now wonderfully 'his old self', as Lydia reported with relief (Moggridge 1992, 615). And Virginia Woolf recorded in her diary:

> Maynard read a very packed profound and impressive paper so far as I could follow, about Cambridge youth; their philosophy; its consequences; Moore; what it lacked; what it gave. The beauty and unworldliness of it. I was impressed by M. and felt a little flittery and stupid. Then he had to rest; it turned grey and cold. ... Nevertheless a very human satisfactory meeting. Tea: Lydia presiding,

'Now boys and girls sit down'. Hot cakes. Ham
sandwiches. No politics. (VWD 5:168–9)

The politics were surely between the lines. Keynes
said in his paper: 'And as the years wore on towards 1914, the
thinness and superficiality, as well as the falsity, of our view
of man's heart became, as it now seems to me, more obvious' (JMK 10:449). In context, it seems evident that this was
directed at Woolf: that Keynes chose to give, not a faithful
description of his own state of mind before 1914, but a sad
and gentle rebuke to Woolf's state of mind at the height of
the Czechoslovak crisis. It could hardly have been orches-
trated more tellingly. And it was precisely because he shared
so many of her values that he exploited the conventions – and
the camaraderie – of the Memoir Club to convey his point in
this subtle, civilised, non-confrontational way.

Virginia Woolf surely realised this. Three weeks afterwards, the immediate crisis had been defused. Chamberlain
and Hitler had met at Munich, their agreement to dismember
Czechoslovakia famously inscribed on a sheet of paper put into
Chamberlain's hand; but war averted for the moment. 'The
Keyneses to tea yesterday', Virginia recorded on 3 October.
'All a put up job between Chamberlain & Hitler, Maynard
said. Never had been any chance of war'. This was all highly
implausible, of course, on the true import of the international
situation; but the domestic scene was more tranquil. 'M. &
Lydia very congenial – dear old M. so sanguine, so powerful,
somehow lovable too, and Lord how brilliant. I kissed him.
Hope all is forgotten and forgiven' (VWD 5:179).

***

Either before the First World War or before the Second, it is implausible to convey a picture of Keynes's concerns and preoccupations while ignoring a strong political element. The fact that the Liberal Party into which he had, in effect, been born in Harvey Road had, by the 1930s, descended into ideological factionalism and parliamentary impotence did not undermine the validity of liberalism in Keynes's eyes. A temperamental optimist and a political pragmatist, he looked for allies wherever he could find them – and sometimes hopefully discerned promising ideological affinities waiting to be liberated from the shackles of factional partisanship.

Kingsley Martin, who knew him well, surely knew what to expect when he recruited Keynes for one of a series of conversations published in the *New Statesman* in early 1939. As editor and interlocutor, Martin had already engaged with Herbert Morrison of the Labour Party, as well as with the two great rogue figures of British politics, Lloyd George and Churchill. It was not simply Martin's own long-standing respect for his Cambridge mentor (nor even the obvious fact that Keynes was virtually Martin's boss at the *New Statesman*) that inspired this editorial decision to give the author of the *General Theory* the same sort of platform to advertise his political views. What Keynes said would hardly have come as a surprise to those who knew him, echoing his long-held views about a progressive ideological affinity between Liberals and Labour, albeit often thwarted by the competitive imperatives of the British electoral system; and likewise that a supposed dichotomy between 'capitalism' and 'socialism' was largely a redundant rhetorical legacy.

'Most politicians are committed either to the view that private capitalism works very well as it is, or to the view that it should be got rid of altogether', Keynes argued. 'From the days when I served on the Liberal Industrial Inquiry, I have felt that there was too little organised sympathy for attempts to make the private property system work better' (JMK 21:492–3). The *General Theory* was now tacitly the handbook he offered for achieving this economic objective; but Keynes preferred to appeal to history. He invoked a long pedigree for the notion that a right to property was a legitimate pillar of liberalism, though one that had often been corrupted – perniciously, by lawyers, he suggested – into a defence of vested interests. In Keynes's view, then, 'the real convictions of at least three-quarters of the country today are in the most fundamental and genuine meaning of the word, liberal. Indeed, it is this which explains the unreality of contemporary party politics' (JMK 21:494).

Keynes's expansive list of liberals now included most Conservative and Labour politicians. 'Mr Lloyd George is a good enough liberal himself', he conceded. Churchill was likewise claimed as a liberal; Morrison and Attlee too. 'The real obstacle lies in our not having a Government of that complexion'. Keynes dropped other names, teasingly including Martin himself, though explicitly excluding Shaw. 'There is no one in politics today worth sixpence outside the ranks of liberals except the post-war generation of intellectual Communists under thirty-five. Them too I like and respect'. In particular, Keynes derided the official line of the Labour Party: 'Why cannot they face the fact that they are not sectaries of an outworn creed mumbling moss-grown demi-semi-Fabian Marxism, but the heirs of eternal liberalism, whose sincere convictions reflect and should inspire those of the great majority of their countrymen?' (JMK 21:494–5).

Much of this was simply an updated rendering of the sort of political analysis that Keynes had offered since the mid-1920s, when the factional in-fighting and electoral collapse of the Liberal Party had resulted in a new two-party system, in practice favouring the Conservatives. But in January 1939 the newly topical element was an initiative launched within the Labour Party, and headed by one of its most prominent figures, Sir Stafford Cripps, a brilliant and well-remunerated lawyer, with a history of maverick left-wing interventions (also a nephew of Beatrice Webb). Cripps's current ploy was his campaign for a Popular Front, aimed at uniting Labour with the non-socialist left in the post-Munich situation, in order to displace the Chamberlain government. 'I am all for Sir Stafford Cripps, and I would join his movement if he is successful in getting it launched', Keynes now told Martin in his *New Statesman* interview (JMK 24:496).

One of Cripps's prominent supporters in his new movement was Lady Violet Bonham Carter, Asquith's daughter, a loyal Liberal and a long-standing friend of Churchill. She now applauded the fact that Keynes had given public support and was (she wrote) impressed that he sent Cripps a cheque for £50 (say, £2,000 or so in today's money) which Keynes had offered along with the advice to Cripps that 'it is hopeless to try to form a new movement as distinct from capturing old ones' (JMK 24:503). And so it proved, since Cripps's initiative had the immediate effect of getting him expelled from the Labour Party in May 1939; though this did not deter Cripps in

195

the following month from opening a private line to a similarly threatened rebel member of the Conservative Party, Winston Churchill. Both were to find their political fortunes transformed by the coming of the Second World War; and much the same could be said of Keynes himself.

Moreover, there was one respect in which these political issues had a very direct and significant economic dimension. In response to the worsening international situation, the Chamberlain government stepped up its rearmament programme. In May 1939 Keynes spoke on BBC radio about the implications for unemployment. He asked whether 'for reasons beyond our control, the grand experiment is to be made. In rearming this country, shall we, by accident so to speak, cure unemployment?' (JMK 21:528). Rehearsing arguments that he had refined over the previous fifteen years, since his first public contentions that prosperity might be cumulative, he surveyed the impact of this increased expenditure, given that the Chancellor of the Exchequer had decided that it would not be offset by taxation. He estimated, on a conservative basis, that 'the direct effect of the armament expenditure may be to take 300,000 off the dole' (JMK 21:531).

If this was the first part of the story that Keynes told, it was the further impact that now, in simple terms, demonstrated the secondary effect of new spending by those newly employed. 'By how much will this second effect multiply the first effect?' he asked. 'It is not easy to say. We have only lately begun to look at the problem just this way, and the statisticians have not yet collected enough material for a safe forecast'. Here was the practical test of his own recent theory, explicitly termed as 'the multiplier effect' and, according to his estimates, capable of producing a total increase of employment of perhaps 500,000. 'If it works, if expenditure on armaments really does cure unemployment, I predict that we shall never go back all the way to the old state of affairs. If we can cure unemployment for the wasted purposes of armaments, we can cure it for the productive purposes of peace' (JMK 21:531–2). For Keynes, the temperamental optimist, the looming clouds of the Second World War revealed this silver lining. In due course, he was indeed provided with an opportunity to work in the Treasury – among some old friends, and in a role that now allowed him to exert power circumscribed by necessity.

9

The Road to Bretton Woods
Expediency Revisited

In his generous obituary notice of Keynes in 1946, his great Austrian-American rival Joseph Schumpeter wrote that 'Keynes's advice was in the first instance always English advice, born of English problems even when addressed to other nations' (Schumpeter 1952, 274–5). This observation is often worth bearing in mind when reading Keynes's writings, even where these purport to offer an objective analysis of general economic problems, as in his two major works of economic theory. His *Treatise on Money* (1930) was quite unlike his earlier *Treatise on Probability* (1920) in style: no longer a fastidious and mathematically challenging exposition of formal propositions but instead a literary *tour de force*, where invention, parables and mischief often rescue, through diverse insights, some weaknesses in the overall argument. For the work can indeed be read as a vast generalisation of Keynes's polemical indictment of the high rates of interest set by the Bank of England in the 1920s, under the unforgiving harrow of the gold standard, thus producing a *disequilibrium* that manifested itself in high unemployment. And then the *General Theory* (1936) turned the logic of this central message around by suggesting that 'equilibrium' itself could be the real problem – if it described an economy (that was all too like Britain's) locked into a sub-optimal stasis. Each of these formal economic works, then, advanced generalisations, as Schumpeter was not alone in suggesting, that often seemed uncannily supportive of Keynes's current and specific policy objectives, and seen through spectacles 'made in England'.

If such charges can be levelled with some plausibility against Keynes's major theoretical books, it might well alert us to hunt the (nationalistic) sub-text in his practical policy advice too. What Keynes wrote about the international gold standard in the inter-war years was obviously influenced by the link that he saw with British unemployment. Playing by the rules of the gold standard had, in effect, entailed a sacrifice necessitated by the vanity project of sustaining sterling at an internationally uncompetitive level. And when Keynes became a prestigious advisor to the British Treasury in the desperate war situation of 1940, he inevitably brought with him his reputation as a renowned critic of the inter-war gold standard.

It may be no surprise, then, to find him in due course becoming the spokesman for plans to remodel the post-war international currency system – an enterprise that formed the agenda for the great conference held at Bretton Woods in 1944. This was what subsequently made the name of this small, peaceful mountain resort town in New Hampshire as universally recognisable as evocative place-names like Stratford-on-Avon or Gettysburg or indeed Bloomsbury. The eponymous significance of 'Bretton Woods' rests on the claim that this marked the inception of a new era in international economic policy, notably through creating institutions – the World Bank and the International Monetary Fund – that were to recast global trade and currency relations. Yet no less than with 'Yalta', after the Big Three held their notorious meeting in the Crimea a few months later, 'Bretton Woods' was a reflection of the current state of relations between the victorious Allies, and of their relative power at the time. The D-Day landings in Normandy by American and British Commonwealth and Empire forces had been accomplished in June 1944, and though the military outcome in Europe hung in the balance while the Bretton Woods conference deliberated during July, this was ostensibly a high moment in Anglo-American cooperation.

The hosts at Bretton Woods were not the US State Department, under its Secretary of State, the ideological free-trader Cordell Hull. Instead, Hull was deliberately excluded and the US Treasury had taken charge. Its Secretary, Henry Morgenthau, a close confidant of President Roosevelt, was accordingly given a high honorific role in presiding at the conference. But in personal terms everyone agreed that the work was dominated by two figures.

One was Harry White for the US Treasury: an economist himself, very able, trusted by Morgenthau, a committed New Dealer and (as we now know) a fellow-traveller who was passing sensitive information to the Soviet Union (Steil 2013, 4–6). The other was Lord Keynes of Tilton (as he had become in 1942) as head of the UK delegation, supported in his now precarious medical condition by Lady Keynes. His actual governmental position was almost impossible to define; he had no rank, he took no salary – his personal income was always above £11,000 per annum in the war years (say, £600,000 today) (JMK 12:2). He was 'just Keynes', licensed to intervene where he chose but obviously bound here by his official brief.

And of course he was now the most famous economist in the world. He was more famous than Schumpeter or Hayek, certainly more famous than White; indeed White had to endure US press comment that he was in awe of Keynes. One observer at Bretton Woods said: 'The happiest moment in the life of Harry White came when he could call Keynes by his first name' (Gardner 1980, 111).

Maybe. It is more sobering to explore the context in which a Keynes Plan, and then a rival White Plan, had been formulated; and how the two of them came to agree on the common proposals that became the agenda for Bretton Woods in 1944. For as early as 1941, Keynes had formulated his views on what he initially called an International Currency Union – a name changed in his later drafts in 1942 to International Clearing Union. The proposal in these drafts that some sort of international currency should be created – this was to be called 'bancor' – has received subsequent attention, most recently in the era of the euro when some of the issues raised, about international equilibrium and the impact of making settlements between creditor countries and debtor countries, are intrinsically similar. Likewise, the name of the Polish economist Michal Kalecki is today well known to economists who grapple with the continuing problems that face developing countries over linked issues of foreign investment and the terms on which they trade internationally. The fact that Kalecki, who had independently formulated a concept of effective demand in the early 1930s, was sympathetic in 1943 to Keynes's 'bancor' proposals – as he made clear from his wartime base in Oxford – is no surprise and rightly attracts attention today when such issues are discussed.

But if we are trying to understand the bearing of the Keynes Plan on the outcome at Bretton Woods, the significant point is that 'bancor' did not form part of the proposals put to the conference. When Keynes outlined the agenda for Bretton Woods to the House of Lords before he left for the United States in May 1944, he made light of this by saying 'there is no longer any need for a new-fangled international monetary unit. Your Lordships will remember how little any of us liked the names proposed – bancor, unitas, dolphin, bezant, daric and heaven knows what'. As Keynes put it, 'it has been the dog that died' (JMK 26:10).

But this was not actually a laughing matter. If a new international currency was not needed, why not? Long ago, in the *Treatise on Money* in 1930, Keynes had offered the sly speculation that, in any projected reform, 'if we could once overcome the many obstacles in the way of a scientifically managed world system, it would not add much to our difficulties to give it a gold camouflage' (JMK 6:268). Can we infer, then, that this later became his strategy at Bretton Woods? Conversely, might it mean that Bretton Woods was actually a great camouflage operation for restoring the gold standard? Keynes repeatedly denied this, appealing to his own track record as a notorious critic of the gold standard – an effective rhetorical point but not perhaps the end of the argument. The fact was that much in the Keynes Plan of 1943 had meanwhile been subsumed or subverted within an agreed compromise that was much closer to the American White Plan. And the responsibility for this reorientation lay with Keynes himself, now acting not as an economist so much as an emissary of the increasingly beleaguered British government, with its dependence on American support ever more evident as the war took its toll on the British economy.

***

Keynes's starting point in 1941 had inevitably been to describe and to understand the gold standard. Why, in particular, had the gold standard not worked in the inter-war years? To Keynes, as we have seen in Chapter 6, it now seemed obvious that the United States was the natural successor to Britain as the major creditor nation, so it ought (as we would now put it) to have assumed an active hegemonic role, meaning (as Keynes put it at the time) that it ought to have played by the rules of the game in actively recycling its surpluses. Perhaps the American lack of an active central bank – with the Federal Reserve system still in its infancy in the 1920s – was an unspoken issue here. The fact was that, rather than letting cheap money and inflation adjust dollar prices, tight monetary policy had been maintained in the United States. This had an inhibiting effect upon American investment overseas, keeping the money at home, ultimately symbolised in the vast accumulation of bullion at Fort Knox, Tennessee.

The conventional American view was naturally more complacent – just as the conventional British view had once been, of course, in the days of British hegemony. Moreover, it was American policy that was now likely to prevail and the Second World War gave the State Department under Cordell Hull greater scope to apply it. In particular, two pre-war grudges against Britain still loomed large. One was that Britain manipulated its currency after the 1931 crisis took the pound off the gold standard, thus in effect devaluing it against the dollar and giving sterling an unfair trading advantage. This must stop, Hull insisted.

The second American grievance was that the British had likewise manipulated trade, notably with their own Empire and Commonwealth (as the self-governing Dominions were now termed). In particular the Ottawa agreements of 1932, negotiated in the Canadian capital, had instituted a system of imperial preference between the different parts of the Empire: not only the colonies but especially the self-governing Dominions. This was actually a desperate measure in a crisis, but the policy enjoyed strong ideological support from the Conservative Party in Britain, which had long campaigned for preferential tariffs to bind together the Empire. Here was a sentiment stronger at the grassroots than in the leadership, but always capable of being roused. The notion that there were immense opportunities for bilateral trade deals between Britain and the countries of white settlement in the Commonwealth remained potent, with long-lasting echoes even today.

Keynes had turned against gold in the early 1920s when British experience revealed to him the iron hand beneath the velvet glove. Countries in deficit were *forced* to use high interest rates to bring down prices, at a domestic cost of unemployment. Countries in surplus had the *option* of lower interest rates; but might instead choose to use their creditor status to amass their gold in bank vaults (or later at Fort Knox) rather than recycling it. Hence there was a deflationary bias in the system as a whole because the rules of the game were asymmetrical in effect, forcing policies upon deficit countries that could only result in high unemployment. And, of course, even in Keynes's first book on Indian currency in 1913, his scorn at the fetish of locking up gold reserves rather than using them is already apparent.

It was in the *Treatise on Money* in 1930 that Keynes formally set out his critique and his suggestions for remedy: all framed in terms of Burkean expediency rather than Jacobin zeal. He had argued that 'there are great and obvious advantages in retaining gold as our international standard, provided, as we have previously expressed it, that we can retain the metal as a constitutional monarch, wholly subject to the will of a cabinet of central banks who would hold the supreme power'. If this was the conservative aspect of the argument, it was the current world economic crisis that suggested that 'the public opinion of the world may be getting readier to consider with a friendly eye proposals for radical change, than it was in 1925' (JMK 6:348–9). Hence his proposals for 'supernational management' and a 'supernational bank', favouring some inflation that would lessen the burden of past debts and thus 'loosen the grip of the dead hand' (JMK 6:353). And the process should be incremental, relying less upon 'the terms of a paper constitution' and more upon 'the exercise of daily wisdom by the monetary authorities of the world' (JMK 6:360).

It is worth noting that Keynes's first biographer, Roy Harrod, in his summary of the *Treatise*, chose to reproduce three extensive passages dealing, respectively, with its analysis of the weaknesses of the international gold standard; with its case for a supernational authority; and with its extenuation of the United States and France for allegedly breaking the rules of the game in (legitimate) pursuit of their own national interest (Harrod 1951, 410–12). These understandably seemed salient points to Harrod since he was himself prominent in developing a similar analysis in the 1930s. He had identified a deflationary bias in the world economy that needed international corrective action; and this helps explain Harrod's subsequent close collaboration over the Keynes Plan (Pérez Caldentey 2019, 304–5). Given his own learning curve, then, it is not surprising that Keynes's starting point in thinking about post-war currency relations was to devise a system with a mild inflationary bias, worldwide. The objective was to be achieved by recasting the rules of the game so as to make the obligations symmetrical as between creditor and debtor countries.

Moreover, this surely reflects the essence of Keynes's outlook as a political economist. He was, as we have seen in earlier chapters, never just an academic economist but one who made frequent interventions in policy debates from 1913 onward: on the gold standard and India, on reparations and the Versailles Treaty, on Britain's return to gold in 1925, on the need for a stimulus to the British economy in the late 1920s, on the 1931 crisis and the right policy for Britain to adopt after leaving the gold standard. In all this, though no cloistered academic, he had been a free agent, speaking for himself as an economist. But we should not lose sight of the fact that from 1940 onward he was also – and increasingly – the economic statesman of a country that still thought of itself as a great power but was simultaneously under constant pressure to accommodate to the views, and to the policies, and to the interests of the United States.

Such pressure could assume many forms, in translating economic hegemony into political potency. Nobody was more aware than Keynes of the way that the Second World War enhanced the world role of the United States, not least through the imperatives of a booming war economy. In the summer of 1940 he had pointed to the immense growth of what we would now call GDP in the United States under the impact of a war that it had not yet joined. He commented (in a widely circulated American magazine): 'It is, it seems, politically impossible for a capitalistic democracy to organize expenditure on the scale necessary to make the grand experiment which would prove my case – except in war conditions' (JMK 22:149–50). By 1945 the GDP of the United States was to exceed its 1940 level by 75 per cent in real terms. The comparable figure for the United Kingdom was virtually nil, despite full employment, since a large proportion of the male workforce was employed unproductively in the armed forces. (Alternatively, one might say that the productive capacity of the war economy had been sustained at its previous level despite military mobilisation.)

The real negative impact of the war was on Britain's external trading position. From early 1941 the British war effort became fundamentally dependent on external economic support from the United States, in the form of Lend-Lease. This was famously characterised by Churchill in a speech in November 1941 as 'a majestic policy' that was 'dedicated to the cause of world freedom without – mark this for it is unique – the setting up of any account in money', thus making it 'the most unsordid act in the whole of recorded history' (Clarke 2007, 11). And there is no need to mock this, either what Roosevelt did or what Churchill said; but there is rather more to the story than these fine sentiments.

Lend-Lease was one of two crucial turning points in Britain's war – fully as important as June 1941 when Russia came into the war following Hitler's invasion; and more important, in this perspective, than the United States's formal entry as a belligerent in December 1941. In geopolitical military terms, Britain's role in the world war was now no longer crucial, as it had been in 1940; but in national economic terms Britain's dependence on sustaining American goodwill became more and more obvious from early 1941 onwards.

Keynes was in a particularly good position to appreciate this since he was sent to Washington in the summer of 1941, staying there for three months (with Lydia's now indispensable support in accompanying him) on a rather frustrating mission to understand US policy. The idea of Lend-Lease had initially been formulated by Roosevelt himself in vague but visionary terms which indeed included a plea to 'get rid of the silly, foolish old dollar sign' in the material aid that was given. But the political process of passing the necessary Bill through Congress produced a more pragmatic outlook. Keynes met Morgenthau and reported back to London in May 1941 that 'we also discussed the question of what is called here "consideration". That is to say the ultimate terms of settlement of the Lend Lease Bill and the sort of return we are to be expected to make in respect of it' (JMK 23:86).

This seems a very odd way of putting the matter – as though Keynes had never heard of this 'consideration' and had to explain it to his own government. It illustrates the fact that the British and the Americans were looking at Lend-Lease through different lenses. The Churchillian rhetoric continued to insist that no 'sordid' motives should be imputed: nothing base, vile, mean, greedy, niggardly, self-interested or purely materialistic. But in American political culture, as Keynes was evidently learning, it was only natural to apply a more transactional standard, with no imputation that there was anything dishonourable about 'a deal'. After all, Roosevelt's whole presidency had been based on the New Deal that he promised.

In a deal, however mutually beneficial it might appear, each party brought something to the table; this was how to make a contract in which the benefit conferred on one side was matched by a benefit, or a 'consideration', promised in reciprocation. Now the historic British way in warfare had used a different sort of vocabulary when offering 'subsidies' to allies whose own armies had often made it unnecessary for the British to deploy their own troops; this was thought of as money well spent, fully recompensed by services in the field in a common cause. Robert Brand, as the British official now responsible for food procurement in Washington under Lend-Lease, naturally understood this; and as a friend of Keynes from the days of the Versailles Treaty, he shared a similar perspective, reinforced by their contacts during Keynes's visit to Washington. As Brand put it: 'Fighting is the real consideration for the whole Lend-Lease Act' (Hopkins 2021, 115).

The American way in warfare, however, was now bound to prevail, and with it the American view of the rationale of Lend-Lease. For what the United States offered was a form of aid ultimately worth many billions of dollars to save the British balance of payments – so what was the *quid pro quo*? When Keynes stumbled over the alien term 'consideration' in May 1941 he was embarking on a learning curve that was to shape virtually everything that he proposed in this field in the five remaining years of his life.

He tried to explain some of this to the House of Lords in December 1945, faced with the final ratification of the Bretton Woods and American Loan agreements: 'How difficult it is for nations to understand one another, even when they have the advantage of a common language. How differently things appear in Washington than in London, and how easy it is to misunderstand one another's difficulties and the real purpose which lies behind each one's ways of solving them'. He drew the conclusion that it was often better to be 'more practical and more realistic – to use two favourite American expressions' in such discussions (JMK 24:606). It would be too simple to suppose that there was a visionary, highly principled Keynes Plan that fell victim to the machinations of American power politics at Bretton Woods. Keynes too was playing for high stakes in both a strategic and a tactical sense, often anticipating American reactions and sensibilities before formulating and reformulating his own proposals.

***

The origins of the Keynes Plan lie in the International Currency Union proposals that he drafted in September 1941 – *after* Lend-Lease had been implemented in practice but *before* the 'consideration' had been legally embodied in Article VII of the formal agreement on Lend-Lease in February 1942. Article VII will resurface in this story. It specified a joint commitment to the 'elimination of all forms of discriminatory treatment in international commerce' after the war. As the Americans understood it, this ruled out imperial preference, which had obviously sanctioned 'discrimination' within the British Empire, encouraging bilateral trade deals within the Commonwealth, notably between Britain and New Zealand, Australia and Canada.

Now bilateralism had been crucial in sustaining the Nazi war economy under Hitler's Finance Minister, Dr Hjalmar Schacht, leading to talk of a 'Schachtian system'. It was his successor Dr Walther Funk who presented the famous 'New Order' for Europe in 1940 at the height of Nazi success in conquering most of western Europe. Its essence was to channel trade via a series of bilateral arrangements whereby goods were essentially bartered, running up credit or deficit balances for the two governments concerned in each of their local currencies, rather than settling by gold transfers. In practice the terms were loaded in favour of Nazi Germany of course; but the *principle* of Schachtianism challenged the whole fabric of the gold standard as a financial means of regulating and equilibrating such transactions. Hence Keynes's private response to the British Ministry of Information in November 1940: 'Well, obviously I am not the man to preach the beauties and merits of the gold standard. ... If Funk's plan is taken at its face value, it is excellent and just what we ourselves ought to be thinking of doing' (JMK 25:2).

Some of this feeling survives in Keynes's first draft of his own plan in September 1941. The last years of the gold standard had seen half-a-dozen false approaches in the quest for equilibrium: perhaps via floating exchange rates, or by competitive deflation, or by competitive devaluations, or by tariffs and discrimination. It was only after these trials and errors, Keynes wrote, that 'Dr Schacht stumbled in desperation on something new which had in it the germs of a good technical idea' – essentially, barter (JMK 25:23). (He evidently harboured no personal animus against Schacht, who had been recruited as a contributor to the *Manchester Guardian* Supplements back in 1922.) Keynes's own critique of the gold standard rested on the fact that the processes of adjustment were not actually symmetrical, because even though 'the social strain of an adjustment downwards is much greater than that of an adjustment upwards', it remained the case that 'the process of adjustment is *compulsory* for the debtor and *voluntary* for the creditor' (JMK 25:28, italics in original).

Through his British spectacles, the gold standard had appeared to Keynes as working benignly enough in the late nineteenth century, under British hegemony, because surpluses had been recycled in overseas investment; the rules of the game had failed under American hegemony, hence Fort Knox as a sterile symbol of international deflation and stagnation. Keynes saw three possible alternatives. 'The United States do not at present favour any radical remedy,' he noted under the first head, having reached this discouraging opinion on any of the American options after spending his three months in Washington. A second possibility was to build on bilateral schemes, whether described in Schachtian terms or in those of imperial preference. Almost by elimination, he came to his own 'ideal scheme which would preserve the advantages of an international means of payment universally acceptable, whilst avoiding those features of the old system which did the damage' (JMK 25:32).

This is the frame for Keynes's International Currency Union proposals. These plainly built upon the principles discussed at length in his *Treatise on Money*, including a revamped 'supernational bank', and embodying the same kind of incremental and pragmatic strategy over implementation. The central aim was to enable countries to clear their accounts on trade on a multilateral basis, in a way functionally similar to the gold standard *when it had worked* – but now with requirements on creditor as well as debtor countries to ensure that it really would function properly. Persistent debtor countries were required to devalue their currency, so no real novelty here; but persistent creditor countries were required to revalue upwards, backed by an ultimate penalty of confiscation of their excess quota by the bank. And nobody would actually use gold in these transactions. 'The *fundamental* provision of the scheme', Keynes wrote in December 1941, 'is the establishment of a Currency Union based on international bank-money, called (let us say) bancor' (JMK 25:72, my emphasis).

There was no need for subscription of the capital of the bank, since it was operating within a closed system, with deposits from some members necessarily balancing overdrafts for others, but increasing international liquidity by the magic of the banking principle. The whole point, reiterated in all the early documents, was clear: to substitute an expansionist in place of a contractionist pressure on world trade. In Keynes's own successive drafts in late 1941, however, one key change was to water down the pressure on a creditor, especially with the removal of any provision for confiscation, and instead simply to rely upon revaluation measures to correct disequilibrium. The main creditor in this era, of course, was the United States; and this is not the only way that

accommodation of specific American concerns and susceptibilities was built in to the process of drafting all along.

As Keynes had said at the outset (8 September 1941):
'it is with this scheme that I should approach the United States.
For it is an attempt to satisfy their fundamental requirements:
it would allow us to subscribe to the blessed word "discrimination"; and it is, therefore, a system in which they might be
more willing to co-operate with enthusiasm' (JMK 25:33). This
comment clearly foreshadows the British signature of Article
VII, the famous 'consideration' for Lend-Lease: no discrimination. Keynes's four drafts from September 1941 to March
1942 were, I suggest, already shaped by this mindset of anticipating and accommodating the American position – whatever that turned out to be. All of this was done by Keynes
before he had seen the White Plan; most of it done before a
White Plan even existed.

***

The origins of the White Plan had come only a week after
the Japanese attack on Pearl Harbor, which had brought
American entry into the war in early December 1941 as a full
belligerent, in Europe as well as in the Pacific theatre. The
instruction came from Morgenthau but the speed of White's
response suggests that he already had some thoughts on the
subject of post-war financial arrangements. His first draft was
ready by the end of December 1941 and discussions took place
within the US Treasury until May 1942.

White worked deliberately without consultation with
the British and, above all, without the *appearance* of any such
consultation. There was no 'special relationship' here; other

American allies were brought into the picture on a par with the British, at least in formal terms. This included Russia, of course, which suited White's general orientation nicely, though it is difficult to identify any particular sinister influence in what was actually done – everyone on the Allied side currently wanted to please Stalin, the master of the Red Army. The Latin American countries were likewise recruited by the United States, as a counterweight to the British Empire. Some on the British side might sneer at these banana republics as puppets, but of course that is exactly how many Americans regarded most of the countries of the British Empire. In almost every draft of the White and Keynes Plans, it turned out that the international voting power of the British Empire and of the United States and its satellites would be equal, or would enable a blocking vote by either one.

In July 1942 a copy of the White Plan was leaked to the British – by White himself, who wanted Keynes to see it and no doubt wished to control this process. Some essential differences of structure and function in the proposals now became clear. White proposed a new institution called the International Stabilisation Fund to deal with international clearing of trade balances. Countries could participate by subscribing set quotas in gold – or in US dollars, which would alone be fully convertible into gold. There was a rather shadowy plan to use a standard unit of account, to be called 'unitas', but since this was created by subscription it was only superficially an equivalent of 'bancor', created out of thin air as bank money. Keynes's private comments indicate his ambivalence. 'Seldom have I been simultaneously so much bored and so much interested', he told his colleagues. 'The general attitude of mind seems to me most helpful and also enlightening. But the actual technical solution strikes me as quite hopeless. He has not seen how to get round the gold standard difficulties and has forgotten all about the useful concept of bank money' (JMK 25:159).

In the course of 1942–3, further drafts of both plans ensued – a total of six or eight in each case. These were now competitive proposals, each angling for wider acceptance not only in Anglo-American terms but among allies worldwide. The United States refused to engage in bilateral talks with the British on the two proposals; instead each Treasury showed its own plan to other allies, not only to Latin American states but also to Russia and China on the American side, and not only to Commonwealth countries but also to European governments in exile on the British side.

In the White Plan, as became increasingly apparent, the link not only with gold but also with the dollar as the only currency fully convertible into gold, was fundamental. In Keynes's summary of the differences of the two plans, as circulated internally to colleagues on 1 March 1943, the three essential differences were (JMK 25:225):

1. The subscription basis of unitas as against bancor's creation of credit.
2. The applications of sanctions or correctives against the weaker party in the White Plan, but also against the stronger party in the Keynes Plan.
3. The emphasis upon stability in the White Plan, but upon an expansionist rationale in the Keynes Plan.

These might be thought incompatible principles. Yet, having acknowledged them, Keynes nonetheless concluded: 'the final results can be dressed up in terms of the language and general set-up of either plan, according to taste'. The outstanding differences in his view were the provisions for exchange control, the adequacy of the quotas and – this was new – 'the workability of the proposed solution for dealing with scarce currencies' (JMK 25:226). This 'scarce currency clause' was a late insertion into the White Plan; but it became a matter of central importance for the British. The point was that only the US dollar was likely to become 'scarce' in the sense that other countries would run out of it, or find themselves unable to meet their liabilities on trade with the United States as the universally acknowledged creditor country.

What action, then, was open to a nation in deficit with the United States? Could it, to save precious dollars, take measures to restrict its American imports? That was surely a shocking example of 'discrimination'! Yet the 'scarce currency' language that White had now introduced seemed to license such steps. This is surely why Harrod, now Keynes's close collaborator, wrote to him with some urgency in March 1943: 'The cardinal point is that the Americans offer us in this what we could never have asked of them in the negotiations *especially after signing Article VII*, namely that we (and other countries) should be allowed to discriminate against American goods if dollars are running short' (JMK 25:227, my emphasis). In 1943 Keynes himself was less persuaded on this point; but Harrod was obviously right that the tactical value of the scarce currency clause to the British was the fact that it came as an *American* proposal. Indeed the clause was to

217

give White a great deal of subsequent embarrassment when he faced persistent criticism of it from the US Congress. It survived on paper in the Bretton Woods agreement, though in practice its objectives were generally achieved by other means – in a context where the truly visionary impact of Marshall Aid was to rescue many European economies.

In April 1943 a newspaper leak precipitated the simultaneous publication of the Keynes Plan by the British government and of the White Plan by the United States. This provoked public debate, including astute analysis from Michal Kalecki and his colleague Ernst Schumacher at the Oxford Institute of Statistics. Their paper, while welcoming the approach of the Keynes Plan, criticised its concentration on equilibration of international transactions on current account, rather than on capital account too, which was vital for promoting investment in developing countries (Toporowski 2018, 130–4). One obvious response – that this was a function delegated to other agencies (what became the World Bank) – does not entirely meet this point. Indeed Keynes's own analysis of how the gold standard had functioned successfully in the late nineteenth century pointed to Britain's hegemonic role in recycling current surpluses into *investments* in countries (many of them colonies) that were relatively undeveloped. This was now past history.

In the present moment, Keynes's attention was focussed elsewhere: on the need to win American support for the problems facing countries with inevitable current account deficits after the war. In a memorandum to a Treasury colleague, explicitly emphasising *"The underlying tactics"* in April 1943, Keynes wrote: 'The real risk is that there will be no plan at all and that Congress will run away from their own proposal. No harm, therefore, at least so it seems to me, if the Americans work up a certain amount of patriotic fervour for their own version. Much can be done in detail hereafter to improve it' (JMK 25:242).

This was what Keynes already conceded in April 1943 and he was accordingly ready to cooperate in producing an agreed synthesis as a joint Anglo-American proposal. Indeed the difficulty here was largely tactical on the part of the Americans since they wished simultaneously to cooperate but to avoid any appearance of collusion with the British. Thus, after much shadow-boxing on both sides, an agreed plan was produced as the agenda for the proposed international conference; and in April 1944 a *Joint Statement by Experts on the Establishment of an International Monetary Fund* was published, with a preface written by Keynes glossing its differences with the earlier Keynes Plan.

For British eyes, Keynes suggested that it was little more than the Keynes Plan in new clothing. True, the proposed International Monetary Fund was not to be a bank but a subscribed fund. 'These two arrangements represent alternative technical set-ups, capable of performing precisely the same functions', Keynes now argued; but the Fund had 'the appearance of being closer to what is already familiar' (JMK 25:437–8). Secondly, in regard to his previous proposals for putting pressure on creditor as well as debtor countries: 'These have been replaced in the new proposal by a different, *but perhaps more far-reaching*, provision with the same object in view' (JMK 25:440, my emphasis). This turned out to be the scarce currency clause, which had assumed by this point a truly heroic projected role in rescuing the new joint proposal from the disabling flaws of the gold standard – and rescuing the British post-war balance of payments too perhaps.

***

It was, then, essentially the White Plan that was proposed at Bretton Woods. In this process, not just 'bancor' but the Keynes Plan itself was the dog that had died, disowned in all but name by its master. In the end, what became the key point for Keynes was the trading principle of multilateralism. He thus opted for the best deal he could currently get for Britain in seizing the benefits of participation in a multilateral system. 'No country has more to gain from it than ourselves', he declared in a letter to *The Times* in May 1944. 'For it is a characteristic of our trade that our important sources of supply are not always our best customers'. He pointed to the historic role of sterling, with its general convertibility, as intrinsic to a system upon which Britain's past prosperity had relied. Hence his warning, making an allusion to Burke: 'To adapt a famous phrase, Schachtian minds ill consort with great Empires' (JMK 26:8–9).

Now this barb was specifically aimed at Thomas Balogh, the Hungarian economist who was a colleague of Kalecki at the Oxford Institute. Throughout the years 1944 to 1946 Balogh was active in advising those critics of Keynes's stance, drawn disparately from the left wing of the Labour Party and the right wing of the Conservative Party, who hankered after bilateral deals, either with socialist economies or within the Commonwealth. It was an unlikely political combination but one that periodically resurfaced in the politics of this period – and surely with parallels that we can see in recent British politics. Once the issue polarised in this way, Keynes's priority was to seek to reconcile multilateralism with his long-standing critique of the gold standard.

Before setting off for Bretton Woods, speaking in the House of Lords on 23 May 1944, Lord Keynes himself presented the agreed agenda as an improvement on the Keynes Plan. 'I dare to speak for the much abused so-called experts', he declared and claimed that the proposal now before them was 'the exact opposite of the gold standard' (JMK 26:19–21). He put this in terms of British interests. First, the value of sterling would be set by internal rather than external criteria; secondly domestic interest rates would be 'as low as suits our own purposes'; and thirdly that 'whilst we intend to prevent inflation at home, we will not accept deflation at the dictate of influences from outside' (JMK 26:16). In this version, control of capital movements and the ability to vary the exchange rate were evidently to take the strain, rather than the resort to deflation. It was a pragmatic acceptance of the best terms on offer in this negotiation.

The plain fact was that the Bretton Woods conference was held on American soil and organised along American lines, including the participation of large numbers of lawyers; and, above all, with a basically American agenda. There was to be no new international currency, still less a system based on the creation of bank money. Instead a gold exchange standard was established with the actual hegemony of the dollar now institutionalised; all other currencies in the system were required to become convertible with a US dollar that was alone formally pegged to gold. Non-discrimination in trade was, of course, a precondition of participation in this system.

221

In private, though sustained and policed as ever by Lydia, Maynard was clearly now in constant danger of over-taxing his fragile health. But in the public sessions he performed with a personal mastery that played to his own gifts, as his fellow economist Lionel Robbins aptly recorded in his diary at the time, writing of an early joint session with the Americans: 'This went very well indeed. Keynes was in his most lucid and persuasive mood; and the effect was irre-sistible'. Robbins was almost as much impressed by Lord Keynes's charismatic performance at Bretton Woods as the young Keynes had once been by Lloyd George's in Paris: 'He uses the classical style of our life and language, it is true, but it is shot through with something which is not traditional, a unique unearthly quality of which one can only say that it is pure genius. The Americans sat entranced as the God-like vis-itor sang and the golden light played around' (Robbins 1990, 158–8). Nobody present would have written in this register about the performative skills of Harry White, but it was his agenda that prevailed at Bretton Woods. When the confer-ence broke up the delegates saluted Keynes by singing 'For He's a Jolly Good Fellow'; but they might as well have sung the more recent ballad 'White Christmas'.

In the geopolitical circumstances of 1944, perhaps a modified White Plan was the most expedient option in res-cuing multilateral trade. But it now came with what looked, in crucial respects, rather like a post-war version of a gold exchange standard: one that still empowered creditor nations to call the shots on how it worked. This seemed entirely natu-ral in American eyes in the 1940s, though rather less so later, with the post-war trading resurgence of Germany, Japan and then China. Indeed, it was by abandoning the dollar's fixed link with gold in 1972 that the Bretton Woods institutions were enabled to survive – but still without reinventing bancor. Wider problems concerning international disparities, which Keynes, like Kalecki, had attempted to address in their own era, have been left as ongoing challenges in the very different world of today.

When two new institutions had been projected – the International Monetary Fund and the World Bank – the British had confidently assumed that the headquarters of one should be in London; but both were assigned to Washington, DC, where, so the British had argued, they would be too much under the political influence of the US government. But that was exactly the point. Moreover, month by month, the British had a poorer hand to play, as they discovered when the obligations they had undertaken at Bretton Woods came to be honoured.

During the later months of 1944 a combination of undue optimism about the war in Europe and undue pessimism about the war in the Pacific theatre stored up important financial and economic consequences for the British. Their current assumption was that American support for the British war effort through Lend-Lease would continue for just a matter of weeks rather than months until German surrender – but with a further long transitional period of perhaps eighteen months before a Japanese surrender, giving plenty of time for these two close Allies to work out their own postwar financial settlement between themselves. As things actually turned out, after a hard winter and an amazing rearguard action by the Germans, VE-Day did not arrive until May

1945; but VJ-Day then came only three months later, once the atomic bombs were dropped at Hiroshima and Nagasaki in August 1945. Roosevelt was now dead; his inexperienced successor President Truman ended Lend-Lease to Britain within a few days.

For the British this acute post-war crisis came more suddenly than anyone had anticipated at the time of the Bretton Woods conference. Keynes called it 'a financial Dunkirk'. He was again sent to the United States (with Lydia) in the autumn of 1945 pleading for further subventions; and what he was offered by the Americans, in the form of a huge dollar loan that was only paid off by the British government in 2006, was hardly what had been envisaged in July 1944. Thus British ratification of the Bretton Woods agreement, notably its conditions for making sterling convertible with the dollar, now became a requisite for Britain getting the necessary dollars. The technical link was that the American Loan agreement stipulated that the Bretton Woods provision for sterling to become freely convertible (in practice into dollars) was now to take place on a fixed and accelerated timetable.

It was thus eighteen months after the New Hampshire conference itself that the final ratification of Bretton Woods, alongside acceptance of the American Loan, had to be agreed. In a tense debate in the House of Lords, Keynes now offered further reasons for accepting the settlement. One of them holds peculiar interest for students of his diverse career, whether in economic theory or in public policy. He now argued that the very economic dominance that the United States enjoyed through the war economy brought with it a process of equilibration. 'Their wages are two and a half times ours', he told the Lords in December 1945. 'These are historic, classical methods by which in the long run international equilibrium will be restored' (JMK 24:623).

Coming from a famous critic of 'the long run' and of 'classical economics', this might seem rather complacent, even though he had made a veiled reference to the options available under the scarce currency clause: 'Both the currency and the commercial proposals are devised to favour the maintenance of equilibrium by expressly permitting various protective devices when they are required to maintain equilibrium and by forbidding them when they are not so required'. And it was in this context that he offered the more ambitious claim: 'Here is an attempt to use what we have learnt from modern experience and modern analysis, not to defeat, but to implement the wisdom of Adam Smith' (JMK 24:621). These were his words at the time; perhaps his actions also drew upon the insights of Smith's contemporary Burke, in bowing to the imperatives of expediency.

Keynes was pictured, sitting inscrutably by the side of Lord Halifax, the British Ambassador to the United States, in signing off the crucial American Loan, perhaps with mixed feelings. Someone at the time had supplied the doggerel lines:

> In Washington Lord Halifax
> Once whispered to Lord Keynes.
> 'It's true they have the money bags
> But we have all the brains.'

Conclusion

Pragmatic and Dogmatic Keynesianism

The experience of the Great Crash of 2008, suddenly blighting the economies of North America and Western Europe alike, had one benign result. It cured any sense of our own superiority to historical experience – as though in the twenty-first century we were immune from unpredictable catastrophes, such as those suffered in Keynes's generation; and perhaps the Covid pandemic further reinforces that message. Though John Maynard Keynes, born in 1883, had a placid childhood in late Victorian England and an early life that he could later recall with sometimes misleading nostalgia, his active career was conducted amid turbulent times. It was crucially punctuated, not only by the Great War that erupted so unexpectedly in 1914, but also successively by the post-war Treaties that left their own scars, by the Great Depression that pulled the whole world into a deflationary downward spiral in the 1930s, and by the catastrophic slide into a Second World War that had only just ended when Keynes died in early 1946, aged only sixty-two.

After his death, the post-war period saw the world remade – and generally for the better, it seemed. One after another, the great European empires were dismantled, sometimes peacefully, more often after debilitating dirty wars, but ushering in an age when international trade boomed. 'Bretton

Woods' lasted through most of three decades, enshrining the dominance of the US dollar, alone tied to gold; and even when this system collapsed in the 1970s, a new regime of floating currencies seemed to function efficiently. Demand management of national economies promoted unprecedented growth, eliminating mass unemployment while generally keeping inflation in check. Thus 'Keynesian' policies, notably in the English-speaking world, appeared to be benignly domesticated for some thirty years after the Second World War. The author's well-known remarks at the conclusion of the *General Theory* now seemed prescient:

> [T]he ideas of economists and political philosophers, both when they are right and when they are wrong, are more powerful than is commonly understood. Indeed the world is ruled by little else. Practical men, who believe themselves to be quite exempt from any intellectual influences, are usually the slaves of some defunct economist. Madmen in authority, who hear voices in the air, are distilling their frenzy from some academic scribbler of a few years back. (JMK 7:383)

Which scribblers, then? If academic economists are asked to name Keynes's real intellectual rivals within their discipline in the twentieth century, they will often mention two figures, both originally Viennese: Joseph Schumpeter, later based at Harvard; and Friedrich von Hayek, successively based in Vienna, at the London School of Economics, in Chicago, and finally back in Salzburg. But in terms of influence, it would be preposterous to ignore the claims of Milton Friedman, an iconic figure in the Chicago school of economics which first challenged Keynesianism in the 1950s and from the 1980s purported to displace it in many American universities.

Some have argued that the post-war Age of Keynes was succeeded in the late twentieth century by the Age of Schumpeter. Certainly there was a major swing in economic fashion by the 1980s, in a world that reeled under inflationary shocks for which Keynesianism was often blamed. On this reading, it was the posthumous triumph of the Schumpeterian vision of 'creative destruction' – a process through which capitalism must be allowed to renew itself without interference or inhibition from government intervention, since the consequential inequities of this process are petty compared with its vast power to enrich the whole community. A similar story, again in counterpoise to Keynes, can be constructed about the reputation of Hayek. His subtle intuitions about the efficacy of market signals, as a vast system for gathering and disseminating more information than any planner could handle, are indeed a central insight. But it took a political revolution in the age of Thatcherism and Reaganomics to provide the ideological context for Hayek's rehabilitation. This belated recognition, it must be said to his credit, was in terms that rather embarrassed the fastidious old man. But perhaps that is the price of fame.

Contemporary economists who have never actually read any of the works of Keynes – or of his great twentieth-century rivals, Schumpeter or Hayek or Friedman – nonetheless confidently invoke their names for their own purposes. Economists thus speak of a Schumpeterian process of creative destruction, or the Hayekian vision of the wisdom of the market, or the Friedmanite view of the power of monetary policy in governing an economy, not by regulating demand but via the supply side. In short, the slaves of these defunct economists use such eponymous labels in a stylised way – as do scientists working in all sorts of different fields, identifying concepts that everyone in the field recognises. I am not going to make a pointless complaint about this sort of professional shorthand, which helps us all to get our bearings quickly, thus avoiding the waste of time and energy involved in reinventing the wheel.

But the question of whether such truths are actually *invented* or whether they are *discovered* is also worth pondering. In this sense, though the paradigm that we now identify for convenience as 'Keynesian' may indeed owe much to his own efforts in conceptualising it, the truths that informed it may have been arrived at, in whole or in part, by others who are now denied the degree of name-recognition that the author of the *General Theory* eventually achieved. Keynes acknowledged this, in his own way, when he wrote the book's penultimate chapter. In it, he saluted historical predecessors who had pointed to 'the inadequacy of the *theoretical* foundations of the *laissez-faire* doctrine upon which I was brought up and which for many years I taught', now bestowing his own overdue tribute to them (JMK 8:339, italics in original). He thus rehabilitated the mercantilists for insights that pragmatic statesmen had always heeded as expedient policy; he defended the rationale of medieval usury laws; he looked with new sympathy at those economists whose work had, as he now saw it, been unjustifiably disparaged within the academic sanctum of orthodox economics. Keynes thus singled out Ricardo's great foe Malthus for resisting the classical school in a previous era.

Among living authors, there was now a notable tribute to J. A. Hobson, a prolific publicist for progressive politics, with a distinctive emphasis on the problem of 'under-consumption' that Keynes had once disparaged. Here were some of 'the brave army of heretics' that the *General Theory* now saluted (JMK 8:371).

If Keynes shocked some academic colleagues with this implied slight upon his own profession, his own claims for the novelty of the *General Theory* occasioned a further kind of professional frisson. For its author seemed chary, or certainly tardy, in crediting forerunners among his fellow academics, notably the 'Stockholm school' of Swedish economists who followed Knut Wicksell (who had died in 1925 and had published mainly in German). Not only Bertil Ohlin but also Gunnar Myrdal felt that Keynes showed 'unnecessary originality' in claims for novel insights that merely showed his ignorance of work not written in English. The contribution of the Danish economist Jens Warming on the multiplier concept was likewise given less recognition than it perhaps deserved; and the pioneering work, published in Polish, by Michal Kalecki on his own theory of effective demand had to await the championship of Joan Robinson to receive due acknowledgement in Cambridge. It can also be said, however, that the logic of 'multiple discoveries' itself lends powerful support to the proposition that such truths lay awaiting discovery (Patinkin 1982, 3–4).

Keynes certainly had a strong sense that he was engaged upon a quest of discovery rather than invention in the *General Theory*; what he invented, perhaps, was his own distinctive way of propagating the truths that he found. He warned in the first words of the preface: 'This book is chiefly addressed to my fellow economists'. Yet in this respect, it sometimes failed; and Frank Knight was not alone among academic economists in finding it an irritating book to read. The reasons for its great impact need to be sought within a wider ambit than that of the economics profession. For when the academic scribblers get their names into wider circulation, the reason is not just intellectual and academic: it concerns *influence*. Economists are influential not just because of their strictly scientific or professional contribution to economics, but often because of a public policy dimension, with an appropriation of their names for vulgarised and simplistic distortions of their original meaning.

Keynes was unusual in that he was not only a great economist but also a figure who was himself persistently active in the realm of public policy. Even here, he remained unusual in that, at various times, he switched between the role of a partisan political propagandist and the vocation of a public servant charged with implementing government policy. And in doing all this, he inhabited a social and intellectual domain – often simply dubbed 'Bloomsbury' – that both shaped and expressed his own values and his own cultural affiliations. It is this virtually unique career, rather than the strait path of a modern economist, that I have sought to sketch in the previous chapters of this book.

***

In the process, I have highlighted certain general concepts. Thus I have sometimes followed Keynes in scrutinising the sense in which truth can be seen as a prime value, especially in formulating and debating public policy. His own actions over the making of the Treaty of Versailles, and then over debating its merits in his *Economic Consequences*, certainly raise some interesting questions – perhaps awkward questions, not least over his own role. Furthermore, the conceptual significance of probability, which had been the focus of his first major academic treatise, also needs to be understood; and the ways in which he modified his own understanding of this concept has pregnant implications for his economic thinking. And then, especially with his increasing exposure in the public policy debates of the 1920s, his long-standing sense of the role for expediency becomes salient. The tension between rules and discretion can help us to understand Keynes's protracted relationship with the international gold standard and likewise his own proposals to replace it in the international monetary system that he envisaged for the world after Bretton Woods.

Keynes had long insisted on the primacy of expediency in seeking to secure current goals, and hence conceived of a wide ambit for political economy, beyond the rigid confines of doctrine or of rule-bound convention. In his *Tract on Monetary Reform* (1924) he argued that the state itself must be free to step outside the contractarian framework, precisely because 'nothing can preserve the integrity of contract between individuals, except a discretionary authority in the state to revise what has become intolerable'. He wrote this in the early 1920s, facing the problem of managing public debt in an era of deflation. But rather than remaining narrowly hedged by the specifics of this particular case, he chose to broaden his ground by asserting a fundamental principle:

'when great decisions are to be made, the State is a sovereign body of which the purpose is to promote the greatest good of the whole. When, therefore, we enter the realm of State action, *everything* is to be considered and weighed on its merits' (JMK 4:56–7, italics in original).

This might well serve as a general liberal axiom; but Keynes, as 'big-L' Liberal, also gave it a more ideological or partisan thrust. He did not initially challenge the theoretical proposition that, in the long run, market forces would produce equilibrium; but he thought it irresponsible simply to sit back idly and wait. As he famously stated: '*In the long run* we are all dead' (JMK 4:65, italics in original). In policy, then, Keynes appealed to social justice and to common sense, faced with real-world imperfections in the market processes – above all because prices were not as flexible as the classical model presupposed. They were, as economists learned to say, sticky in the real world; in particular, wages were sticky when workers refused to take pay cuts. Either 'stickiness' could be bemoaned as a temporary infraction of economic laws; or it could be acknowledged as a real-world constraint on policy options. Keynes, with his practical turn of mind, opted for the latter view.

Keynes's advocacy of public works in Britain from 1924, in a campaign where he now publicly backed Lloyd George, gave him a partisan political image (as a left Liberal). He called for public works as part of a package to administer a stimulus as a means of promoting recovery; and he did so while he was still essentially orthodox in his economic *theory* – what he called 'classical economics'. Liberal individualist doctrine was rejected precisely because it was rooted in fixed assumptions; far from these being immutable, they had simply become obsolete. 'Half the copybook wisdom of our statesmen is based on assumptions which were at one time true, or partly true, but are now less and less true day by day', Keynes declared in his address 'Am I a Liberal?' (1925). 'We have to invent new wisdom for a new age. And in the meantime we must, if we are to do any good, appear unorthodox, troublesome, dangerous, disobedient to them that begat us' (JMK 9:305–6).

Economic liberalism thus had no contractarian sanctity for Keynes but was subject to tests of political expediency in a changing historical context. Within that time-bound context, Keynes was sometimes ready to depict the free market in laudatory terms. His point was not the inherent incapacity of such a system but its current inability to do the job demanded of it. His invocation of the need for state intervention in the 1920s came when, as he perceived it, individualism had failed. As he put it in 1924, in justifying his initial plea for a public works programme: 'we are brought to my heresy – if it is a heresy. I bring in the State; I abandon *laissez faire*, – not enthusiastically, not from contempt of that good old doctrine, but because, whether we like it or not, the conditions for its success have disappeared' (JMK 19:228). Keynes went from bad to worse in the eyes of his critics when he showed himself ready to question, not just the gold standard and the sanctity of a balanced budget, but also the good old Liberal doctrine of Free Trade. On such issues, his own words could often be quoted back against himself. Hence the gibe: 'Where five economists are gathered together, there will be six conflicting opinions and two of them will be held by Keynes!' (Jones 1954, 19).

In short Keynes was ready to abridge 'economic liberalism' in order to achieve full employment if and when – but only when and if – the free market showed itself ineffective in realising this goal. In this he was consistent from the 1920s to the 1940s. The *General Theory* is important to this story not so much in changing the policy agenda as in specifying a different analysis of market failure. Before the inception of the theory of effective demand, Keynes had no theoretical quarrel with the impeccably 'classical' postulate that market-clearing at full employment would take place unless it were impeded by some sort of rigidity, viscosity or obstruction which impeded the fluid and flexible response which was necessary. This is what we can call Pragmatic Keynesianism. And these essentially pragmatic arguments about policy did not demand any conversion to what I distinguish as Dogmatic Keynesianism – using dogmatic in its sense of doctrinal. This doctrinal or theoretical sense of a 'Keynesian revolution' was not propagated publicly until the *General Theory* (1936).

There were, as we have seen, other prominent economists who never became converted to Dogmatic Keynesianism, notably his eminent Cambridge colleagues A. C. Pigou and Dennis Robertson. Yet both Pigou and Robertson had supported Keynes in the years before 1936 over unemployment policy. Others, like Lionel Robbins at the London School of Economics, magnanimously conceded in retrospect that they had been wrong to oppose Keynes in their pragmatic policy advice; but this did not thereby make them into doctrinal or Dogmatic Keynesians. It is clear, then, that Keynes was far from alone as an exponent of Pragmatic Keynesianism, and for the very good reason that adherence to Dogmatic Keynesianism was often not required in order to support the relevance of what he was advocating in public policy.

The year 1933 marked the bottom of the slump – not least the contemporary slump in Keynes's reputation, it could be argued. But in the United States it also saw the election of Franklin Delano Roosevelt as president, proclaiming that there was 'nothing to fear but fear itself'. Keynes warmed to this message and supported FDR's New Deal with its many bold initiatives (some of them contradictory). Indeed ideological opponents denounced him as the evil genius of the New Deal in an alleged slide to socialism. Much has been written about Keynes's supposed influence on FDR – too little perhaps on FDR's influence on Keynes in identifying *confidence* as the key issue. For this became a major theme of the *General Theory* (1936). This is an interesting inversion of the assumption that economic policy is simply a vulgarisation of ideas that derive from economic theory. Or to put the point in the language I am using here, perhaps dogmatic analysis can sometimes derive from insights that are pragmatic in origin.

***

There are really two distinct reasons why Keynes remains relevant today. One is that he can throw us a lifebelt when the ship is sinking. His writings can still suggest to us *how* to save ourselves by resorting to unorthodox measures, notably through fiscal stimulus when the economy faces recession. But reading Keynes may also help us understand *why* the ship started to sink in the first place. In the *General Theory* we are led to understand why – otherwise incomprehensibly – market forces can fail to deliver the goods, can fail to offer self-correction, can fail to cope with a self-inflicted crisis of confidence.

This is a dimension of Keynes's thinking that was largely overlooked in the 'golden age' of Keynesianism after the Second World War. Keynes had a polemical strategy in the *General Theory*, setting up 'classical economics' as his target; and he acknowledged that his friend Robertson had a point in saying that Keynes was assailing a 'composite Aunt Sally of uncertain age' (JMK 14:215). Here the whirligig of time duly brought in its revenges. After Keynes's death the self-appointed keepers of the dogmatic Keynesian flame, not least in Cambridge, showed a jealous zeal that almost snuffed it out. Moreover, the pragmatic 'Keynesianism' that was credited with working wonders in the 1960s – and was then discredited in the 1970s – was itself a composite Aunt Sally of uncertain age. In that era Keynesian demand management was all the rage. 'Fine tuning' of aggregate demand was conceived in simple hydraulic terms, pumping flows around the system, or trading off employment against inflation – the 'Phillips curve' was supposedly the way to read-off the effects. This was a simplistic model which Friedman made the butt of his demolition job on Keynesianism; and the Keynesians of that era cannot escape reproach here.

But the *General Theory* also points to a *psychology* of economic activity as the key to understanding how markets work. One thing that it suggests is that the study of economics is actually bedevilled by radical uncertainty in a way that many orthodox economists have often refused to recognise. Under these conditions, rational behaviour, based on our most reasonable expectations of the future, is simply not enough to save us from irrational outcomes that virtually nobody intended to bring about. Moreover, not only is the 'classical' economics, against which Keynes rebelled, premised on the model of benign rational decision-making: much the same remains true of the 'new classical' analysis of more recent years. Orthodox economists have thus continued to allow for risk only in terms of probabilities that we can cope with, because they can be measured and offset.

The *General Theory* suggests an alternative view. Some of our knowledge of the future is securely founded, some not. Events that are probable (and can thus be measured or estimated or modelled) are not the problem. One crucial distinction is between what is *probable* and what is *uncertain*. Probability, like the toss of a series of coins, can be estimated in a secure way with a few statistics and a bell-shaped curve; risks there may be – but if they are known risks, they can be insured against by those who know.

The mature Keynes tells the alternative story most cogently in the article he wrote explaining himself in 1937. It was his last essay in theoretical economics, as it turned out, which may not justify us in reverentially regarding it as the last word; but certainly as his own. Here Keynes points to 'the fact that our knowledge of the future is fluctuating, vague and uncertain' as a fundamental reason why we cannot make rational predictions about events that are irreducibly in the lap of *uncertainty*, like the chances of the outbreak of a future war. About such non-trivial matters, 'there is no scientific basis on which to form any calculable probability whatever. We simply do not know', he tells us (JMK 14:113–14).

In that case, we are thrown back upon making the best of a bad job on the basis of hunch, common sense, precedent, convention, superstition, magic, whatever. But we can get by – this is real life, after all – if we know what we are doing. And did the 'masters of the universe' on Wall Street or in the City of London, who supposed before 2008 that they had tamed risk through clever programming, know what they were doing? Hardly. But worse than that is not to know that you do not know. From a starting point where the young Keynes had put his trust in truth and probability alike, he had moved latterly into a world that he recognised as beset by fundamental uncertainty.

This may be one important legacy of doctrinal Keynesianism, but not, I think, the only one. For another of the *General Theory*'s organising insights is at least as important: the dichotomy between individual choice and aggregate outcome in a market. The 'paradox of thrift' is certainly one aspect of this problem: the way that a precautionary flight into saving by everyone simultaneously, because it reduces demand in the economy, will reduce the value of the savings too. But Keynes was pointing here to a problem of more general application, which seems to lack an agreed name, though other variants are 'the fallacy of composition' or 'the tragedy of the commons'. So is the 'prisoner's dilemma', of which game theorists have made much in recent years, though it strikes me as a needlessly artificial elaboration of the essential point, which it might need a Ramsey to express in a more vernacular idiom.

A homely example could be the theatre, where we would each get a better view if we stood up, but if all stand up at once we end up, not with a better view, but with less comfort all round. And a fire panic in the theatre is even worse, if we each seek to save ourselves by all rushing for the doors at once. For the fallacy is to suppose that what *each* person can do, *all* can do simultaneously. And that too tells us how and why markets can fail. Here the term 'rational irrationality' has been deployed to good effect (Cassidy 2009, 210). We do not need to categorise individuals as necessarily irrational in their own behaviour. The real dilemma makes us all prisoners of games in which strategies that seem rational to individuals may prove collectively self-defeating. Such insights, in my view, make it highly rewarding to revisit Dogmatic Keynesianism, which was one of my own objectives in a previous book, which accordingly devoted due attention to both the *Treatise on Money* and the *General Theory* (Clarke 2009).

The present book, however, has had much more to say about Pragmatic Keynesianism, and has done so by examining diverse episodes of 'Keynes in action'. In some of these he seems to me to come out quite creditably, as a well-rounded figure coping with difficult problems in a sane and generous spirit; yet in others he comes out rather badly, not least through a capacity for dissimulation that may sometimes seem culpably self-serving. And we certainly need to acknowledge one difficulty in communing with the spirit of a 'timeless Keynes': that he was famous in his own lifetime for changing his mind. If he was challenged, his reply was: 'When the facts change, I change my mind – what do you do, sir?' Conversation in the 1980s with James Meade, an old member of the 'circus' of 1930–1, is my own source for this remark (which has sometimes been doubted as authentic). What is certainly true is that nobody was less bound by orthodoxies than Keynes. He was always ready to abandon old ideas – including his own – when he came up with better ones: either better suited to changing conditions (mainly in policy) or better in logic and insight (mainly in theory). And he shamelessly stole good ideas from others.

I think it may be a mistake simply to celebrate Dogmatic Keynesianism at the expense of Pragmatic Keynesianism, if only because Keynes himself inserted into his doctrines so much of his own pragmatism. In his essay on Marshall, Keynes approvingly quoted from his old teacher's inaugural lecture: 'I do not assign any universality to economic dogmas. It is not a body of concrete truth, but an engine for the discovery of concrete truth' (JMK 10:196). In his ultimate rejection of 'classical economics', Keynes may himself have proved a heretic but he never set up as the pope of a new religion. After the *General Theory*, he applauded constructive critics who had read it in their own distinctive ways, and he surely did so because he saw that they had engaged in good faith with his arguments, because their minds too were now buzzing with his ideas, and because they too were engaged with the awkward questions that he had irreverently posed. In 1944 on a visit to Washington, DC, after one dinner where he was lionised by an admiring throng of younger American economists, Keynes said at breakfast the next morning: 'I was the only non-Keynesian there' (Hutchison 1977, 58). It was a wry remark but surely a very pragmatic observation.

Ayerst, David (1971), *Guardian: Biography of a Newspaper* (London).

Backhouse, Roger E. and Bradley Bateman (eds.) (2006), *The Cambridge Companion to Keynes* (Cambridge).

Baruch, Bernard M. (1920), *The Making of the Reparation and Economic Sections of the Treaty* (New York and London).

Baruch, Bernard M. (1960), *The Public Years* (London).

Bateman, Bradley (1996), *Keynes's Uncertain Revolution* (Ann Arbor).

Birdsall, Paul (1941), *Versailles Twenty Years After* (London).

Boemeke, Manfred, Gerald D. Feldman and Elisabeth Glaser (eds.) (1998), *The Treaty of Versailles: A Reassessment After 75 Years* (Cambridge); especially essays by the editors; David French; Lawrence E. Gelfand; Anthony Lentin; Niall Ferguson; William R. Keylor; William C. Widenor; Michael Graham Fry; and Gordon Martel.

Brooke, Christopher (1993), *A History of the University of Cambridge, vol. 4: 1870–1990* (Cambridge).

Bunselmeyer, Robert E. (1976), *The Cost of the War, 1914–1919: British Economic War Aims and the Origins of Reparation* (Hamden, CT).

Burnett, Philip Mason (1940), *Reparation at the Paris Peace Conference – From the Standpoint of the American Delegation*, 2 vols. (New York).

Carabelli, Anna M. (1988), *On Keynes's Method* (London).

Carabelli, Anna M. and Mario Cedrini (2010), 'Global Imbalances, Monetary Disorder, and Shrinking Policy Space: Keynes's Legacy for Our Troubled World', *European Journal of Economics and Economic Policies*, 7:303–23.

Carabelli, Anna M. and Mario Cedrini (2014), 'A Methodological Reading of Economic Consequences of the Peace', in Jens Hölscher and Mattias Klaes (eds.), *Keynes's Economic Consequences of the Peace: A Reappraisal* (London), pp. 97–115.

Cassidy, John (2009), *How Markets Fail: The Logic of Economic Calamities* (London and New York).

Clarke, Peter (1988), *The Keynesian Revolution in the Making, 1924–36* (Oxford).

Clarke, Peter (1993), 'Churchill's Economic Ideas, 1900–1930', in Robert Blake and Wm. Roger Louis (eds.), *Churchill* (Oxford), pp. 79–95.

Clarke, Peter (2002), *The Cripps Version: The Life of Sir Stafford Cripps* (London).

Clarke, Peter (2007), *The Last Thousand Days of the British Empire* (London and New York).

Clarke, Peter (2015), 'The Making and Remaking of "Common Sense" about British Economic Policy', in Chris Williams and Andrew Edwards (eds.), *The Art of the Possible: Politics and Governance in Modern British History* (Manchester), pp. 16–31.

Clarke, Peter (2017), *The Locomotive of War: Money, Empire, Power and Guilt* (London and New York).

Clavin, Patricia (2013), *Securing the World Economy: The Reinvention of the League of Nations, 1920–1946* (Oxford).

Cox, Michael (2019), *The Economic Consequences of the Peace* (Switzerland).

Deutscher, Patrick (1990), *R.G. Hawtrey and the Development of Macroeconomics* (London).

Dimand, Robert W. (1988), *The Origins of the Keynesian Revolution* (London).

Dimand, Robert W. and Harald Hagemann (eds.) (2019), *The Elgar Companion to John Maynard Keynes* (Cheltenham and Northampton, MA).

Eatwell, John, Murray Milgate and Peter Newman (eds.) (1987), *The New Palgrave: A Dictionary of Economics*, 4 vols. (London).

Eichengreen, Barry (1990), *Elusive Stability: Essays in the History of International Finance, 1919–39* (Cambridge).

Eichengreen, Barry (1992), *Golden Fetters: The Gold Standard and the Great Depression, 1919–39* (Oxford).

Fitzgibbons, Athol (1988), *Keynes's Vision: A New Political Economy* (Oxford).

Fitzhardinge, L. F. (1979), *The Little Digger, 1914–1952: William Morris Hughes, a Political Biography*, vol. 2 (London and Sydney).

Fletcher, Gordon (2000), *Understanding Dennis Robertson: The Man and His Work* (Cheltenham and Northampton, MA).

Gardner, Richard N. (1980), *Sterling-Dollar Diplomacy in Current Perspective*, new expanded edn (New York).

Gilbert, Martin (1966), *The Roots of Appeasement* (London).

Gillies, Donald (2006), 'Keynes and Probability', in Roger E. Backhouse and Bradley Bateman (eds.), *The Cambridge Companion to Keynes* (Cambridge), pp. 199–216.

Gomes, Leonard (2010), *German Reparations, 1919–32: A Historical Survey* (London).

Groenewegen, Peter (1995), *A Soaring Eagle: Alfred Marshall, 1842–1924* (Aldershot and Brookfield, VT).

Guhin, Michael A. (1972), *John Foster Dulles: A Statesman and His Times* (New York).

Hancock, W. K. and Van Der Poel, Jean (eds.) (1966), *Selections from the Smuts Papers*, vol. 4 (Cambridge).

Hill, Polly and Keynes, Richard (eds.) (1989), *Lydia and Maynard: Letters between Lydia Lopokova and John Maynard Keynes* (London).

Hopkins, Michael F. (ed.) (2021), *British Financial Diplomacy with North America, 1944–1946*, Royal Historical Society, Camden 5th series, vol. 62 (Cambridge).

House, Edward M. (1928), *The Intimate Papers of Colonel House, Arranged as a Narrative by Charles Seymour*, vol. 4 (New York).

House, Edward M. and Seymour, Charles (eds.) (1921), *What Really Happened at Paris* (London).

Hull, Isabel V. (2014), *A Scrap of Paper: Breaking and Making International Law During the Great War* (Ithaca, NY).

Hutchison, T. W. (1977), *Keynes versus the 'Keynesians'...?* (London).

Jones, Thomas (1951), *Lloyd George* (Oxford).

Jones, Thomas (1954), *A Diary with Letters, 1931–1950* (Oxford).

Kahn, Richard (1984), *The Making of Keynes' General Theory* (Cambridge).

Keynes, Geoffrey (1981), *The Gates of Memory* (Oxford).

Keynes, Milo (ed.) (1975), *Essays on John Maynard Keynes* (Cambridge).

Lee, Hermione (1996), *Virginia Woolf* (London).

Lentin, Antony (1985), *Guilt at Versailles: Lloyd George and the Pre-history of Appeasement* (London).

Lentin, Antony (2001), *Lloyd George and the Lost Peace: From Versailles to Hitler, 1919–40* (London).

Lentin, Antony (2004), 'Maynard Keynes and the "Bamboozlement" of Woodrow Wilson: What Really Happened at Paris?', *Diplomacy and Statecraft*, 15(4):725–63.

Light, Alison (2008), *Mrs Woolf and the Servants: An Intimate History of Domestic Life in Bloomsbury* (London).

Link, Arthur S. (1992), trans. and ed. with Manfred F. Boemeke, *The Deliberations of the Council of Four: Notes of the Official Interpreter, Paul Mantoux*, 2 vols. (Princeton).

Lloyd George, David (1938), *The Truth about the Peace Treaties*, 2 vols. (continuous pagination) (London), cited as *TPT*.

Lloyd George, David (1938), *War Memoirs*, 2 vols. (continuous pagination, London; first published 1933–6), cited as *WM*.

Lubenow, W. C. (1998), *The Cambridge Apostles, 1820–1914: Liberalism, Imagination, and Friendship in British Intellectual and Professional Life* (Cambridge).

MacMillan, Margaret (2001), *Peacemakers: The Paris Conference of 1919 and Its Attempts to End War* (London).

Mantoux, Étienne (1946), *The Carthaginian Peace: Or the Economic Consequences of Mr Keynes* (Oxford).

Martin, Kingsley (1969), *Father Figures: A First Volume of Autobiography, 1897–1931*; and *Editor: A Second Volume of Autobiography, 1931–45* (Harmondsworth).

Misak, Cheryl (2020), *Frank Ramsey: A Sheer Excess of Powers* (Oxford).

Moggridge, D. E. (1972), *British Monetary Policy, 1924–31: London The Norman Conquest of $4.86* (Cambridge).

Neu, Charles E. (2015), *Colonel House: A Biography of Woodrow Wilson's Silent Partner* (Oxford).

Nicolson, Harold (1933), *Peacemaking 1919* (London, 1964 reprint).

O'Donnell, R. M. (1989), *Keynes: Philosophy, Economics and Politics* (London).

O'Donnell, R. M. (ed.) (1991), *Keynes as Philosopher-Economist* (London).

Patinkin, Don (1982), *Anticipations of the General Theory? And Other Essays on Keynes* (Oxford and Chicago).

Peden, G. C. (2000), *The Treasury and British Public Policy, 1906–1959* (Oxford).

Pérez Caldentey, E. (2019), 'The Reform of the Global Financial Architecture', in *Roy Harrod* (London), pp. 301–47.

Pruessen, Donald W. (1982), *John Foster Dulles: The Road to Power* (New York and London).

Ramsey, F. P. (1931), for 'Truth and Probability' (1926) in R. B. Braithwaite (ed.), *The Foundations of Mathematics and other Logical Essays* (London and New York), pp. 156–98, electronic version.

Robbins, Lionel (1990), *The Wartime Diaries of Lionel Robbins and James Meade, 1943–5*, ed. Susan Howson and Donald Moggridge (London).

Roberts, Richard (2013), *Saving the City: The Great Financial Crisis of 1914* (Oxford).

Rosenfeld, Sophia (2011), *Common Sense: A Political History* (Cambridge, MA).

Rymes, Thomas K. (1989), *Keynes's Lectures, 1932–35: Notes of a Representative Student* (London).

Schuker, Stephen A. (2014), 'J.M. Keynes and the Personal Politics of Reparations', *Diplomacy and Statecraft*, 25(3):453–71.

Schumpeter, Joseph (1952), *Ten Great Economists* (London).

Sharp, Alan (2008), *The Versailles Settlement: Peacemaking after the First World War*, 2nd edn (London).

Simons, H. C. (1936), 'Rules versus Authorities in Monetary Policy', *Journal of Political Economy*, 44:1–30.

Steil, Benn (2013), *The Battle of Bretton Woods* (Princeton).

Steiner, Zara (2005), *The Lights that Failed: European International History, 1919–1933* (Oxford).

Straight, Michael (1983), *After Long Silence* (London).

Tardieu, André (1921), *The Truth about the Treaty* (London).

Tillman, Seth P. (1961), *Anglo-American Relations at the Paris Peace Conference of 1919* (Princeton).

Tooze, Adam (2018), *Crashed: How a Decade of Financial Crises Changed the World* (London and New York).

Toporowski, Jan (2018), *Michal Kalecki: An Intellectual Biography*, vol. 2 (London).

Toye, Richard (2003), 'The Attlee Government, The Imperial Preference System, and the Creation of the GATT', *English Historical Review*, 118:912–39.

Toye, Richard (2005), 'The Trials of a Biographer: Roy Harrod's Life of John Maynard Keynes Reconsidered', in Richard Toye and

Julie Gottlieb (eds.), *Making Reputations* (London and New York) pp. 123–34.

Trachtenberg, Marc (1980), *Reparation in World Politics: France and European Economic Diplomacy, 1916–1923* (New York).

Winch, Donald (2009), *Wealth and Life: Essays on the Intellectual History of Political Economy in Britain, 1848–1914* (Cambridge).

Woolf, Leonard (1960), *Sowing: An Autobiography of the Years 1880 to 1904* (London).

Woolf, Virginia (1938), *Three Guineas* (London).

Woolf, Virginia (2002), *Moments of Being*, new edition ed. Jeanne Schulkind and Hermione Lee (London).

Biographical Works on Keynes

Backhouse, Roger E. and Bateman, Bradley W. (2011), *Capitalist Revolutionary: John Maynard Keynes* (Cambridge, MA).

Barnett, Vincent (2013), *John Maynard Keynes* (London and New York).

Carter, Zachary D. (2020), *The Price of Peace: Money, Democracy, and the Life of John Maynard Keynes* (New York).

Clarke, Peter (2009), *Keynes: The Twentieth Century's Most Influential Economist* (London and New York).

Davenport-Hines, Richard (2015), *Universal Man: The Seven Lives of John Maynard Keynes* (London).

Harrod, R. F. (1951), *Life of John Maynard Keynes* (London).

Moggridge, D. E. (1992), *Maynard Keynes: An Economist's Biography* (London).

Pigou, A. C. (1946), 'John Maynard Keynes', *Proceedings of the British Academy*, 32:394–414.

Robinson, Austin (1947), 'John Maynard Keynes, 1883–1946', *Economic Journal*, 62:1–68.

Skidelsky, Robert (1983), *John Maynard Keynes, vol. 1, Hopes Betrayed, 1883–1920* (London).

Skidelsky, Robert (1992), *John Maynard Keynes, vol. 2, The Economist as Saviour, 1920–37* (London).

Skidelsky, Robert (2000), *John Maynard Keynes, vol. 3, Fighting for Britain, 1937–46* (London).

JMK: with vol. number and page reference:

Donald Moggridge (with Sir Austin Robinson), *The Collected Writings of John Maynard Keynes*, 30 vols. (Cambridge): cited with references to the following volumes:

JMK 1: *Indian Currency and Finance* (1913)

JMK 2: *The Economic Consequences of the Peace* (1919).

JMK 3: *A Revision of the Treaty* (1922).

JMK 4: *A Tract on Monetary Reform* (1923)

JMK 5: *A Treatise on Money: I, the Pure Theory of Money* (1930)

JMK 6: *A Treatise on Money: II, the Applied Theory of Money* (1930)

JMK 7: *The General Theory of Employment, Interest and Money* (1936)

JMK 8: *A Treatise on Probability* (1921).

JMK 9: *Essays in Persuasion* (1931 text, plus later additions)

JMK 10: *Essays in Biography* (1933 text, plus later additions)

JMK 11: *Economic Articles and Correspondence* (academic)

JMK 12: *Economic Articles and Correspondence* (various, academic)

JMK 13: *The General Theory and After, Part I*

JMK 14: *The General Theory and After, Part II*

JMK 15: *Activities, 1906–1914: India and Cambridge*

JMK 16: *Activities, 1914–1919: The Treasury and Versailles*

JMK 17: *Activities, 1920–1922: Treaty Revision and Reconstruction*

JMK 18: *Activities 1922–1932: The End of Reparations*

JMK 19: *Activities 1922–1929: The Return to Gold and Industrial Policy*

JMK 20: *Activities 1929–1931: Rethinking Employment Policies*

JMK 21: *Activities 1931–1939: World Crisis and Policies*

JMK 23: *Activities 1940–1943: External War Finance*

JMK 24: *Activities 1944–1946: The Transition to Peace*

JMK 25: *Activities 1940–1944: The Clearing Union*

JMK 26: *Activities 1941–1946: Bretton Woods and Reparations*

JMK 27: *Activities 1940–1946: Shaping the Post-war World*

JMK 28: *Social, Political and Literary Writings*

JMK 29: *The General Theory and After: A Supplement*

JMK 30: *Bibliography and Index, plus Omissions*

PWW: with vol. number and page reference:

Arthur S. Link (ed.), *The Papers of Woodrow Wilson*, 69 vols. (Princeton University Press, 1966–94).

VWD: with vol. number and page reference: *The Diary of Virginia Woolf*, ed. Anne Olivier Bell, 5 vols. (Penguin edn, 1979–85)